6809

D0350893

**Library**

PHOENIX BAPTIST COLLEGE
13613 N. Cave Creek Rd.
Phoenix, AZ 85022

**Oakland S.C.M.**

LIBRARY

# STUDIES
## IN
## PHILIPPIANS

# STUDIES
# IN
# PHILIPPIANS

RALPH A. HERRING

PHOENIX FIRST PASTORS COLLEGE
13613 N. Cave Creek Rd.
Phoenix, AZ 85022

BROADMAN PRESS
Nashville, Tennessee

Copyright, 1952

BROADMAN PRESS

Nashville, Tennessee

*Printed in the United States of America*

275, JE 52 LHJ

TO

**WILLEEN**

**"TRUE YOKEFELLOW"**

# FOREWORD

## THE SUNDAY SCHOOL TRAINING COURSE

The Sunday School Training Course prepared by the Sunday School Department of the Baptist Sunday School Board is one of the major means of promoting Sunday school work. Its influence is limited only by its use.

The six sections of the course include studies in Bible, doctrines, evangelism, Sunday school leadership and administration, teaching, age group studies, and special studies. The range of the course is broad, for the field of Sunday school work is broad and requires comprehensive and specific training. Sixteen books are required for the completion of each Diploma.

The study of the Training Course is not to be limited to the present Sunday school workers. Most churches need twice as many workers as are now enlisted. This need can be supplied by training additional workers now. Members of the Young People's and Adult classes and older Intermediates should be led to study these books, for thereby will their service be assured. Parents will find help as they study what the Sunday school is trying to do.

SPECIAL NOTE TO INSTRUCTORS:

During your teaching of this book will you check with the Sunday school superintendent and see if an accurate record of training for the workers is kept? If not, please urge him to set up such a file with an associate superintendent of training in charge. File cards for this purpose may be ordered at nominal cost from your nearest Baptist Book Store.

J. N. BARNETTE
*Secretary, Sunday School Department*
*Baptist Sunday School Board*

# DIRECTIONS FOR THE TEACHING AND
# STUDY OF THE BOOK FOR CREDIT

## I. DIRECTIONS FOR THE TEACHER

1. Ten class periods of forty-five minutes each, or the equivalent, are required for the completion of a book for credit.

2. The teacher is given, when requested, an award on the book taught.

3. The teacher shall give a written examination covering the subject matter in the textbook. The examination may take the form of assigned work to be done between the class sessions, in the class sessions, or as a final examination.

EXCEPTION: All who attend all of the class sessions; who read the book through by the close of the course; and who, in the judgment of the teacher, do the classwork satisfactorily may be exempted from taking the examination.

4. Either Sunday school or Training Union credit may be had for the study of this book. Application for Sunday school awards should be sent to the state Sunday School department, for Training Union awards to the state Training Union department where forms may be secured on which to make application. These forms should be made in duplicate and both copies sent.

## II. DIRECTIONS FOR THE STUDENT*

*(\*The student must be fifteen years of age or older to receive Sunday school credit.)*

### 1. *In Classwork*

(1) The student must attend at least six of the ten forty-five-minute class periods to be entitled to take the class examination.

(2) The student must certify that the textbook has been read. (In rare cases where students may find it impracticable to read the book before the completion of

the classwork, the teacher may accept a promise to read the book carefully within the next two weeks.)

(3) The student must take a written examination, making a minimum grade of 70 per cent, or qualify according to *Exception* noted above.

## 2. *In Individual Study by Correspondence*

Those who for any reason wish to study the book without the guidance of a teacher will use one of the following methods:

(1) Write answers to the questions printed in the book, or

(2) Write a development of the chapter outlines.

In either case the student must read the book through.

Students may find profit in studying the text together, but where awards are requested, individual papers are required.

All written work done by such students on books for Sunday school credit should be sent to the state Sunday school secretary. All of such work done on books for Training Union credit should be sent to the state Training Union secretary.

# CONTENTS

# PLEASE READ THIS FIRST

It will help you to understand chapter 1 if you keep in mind that the author's main purpose is to create a mood. He says: "Because feeling contributes to this effect more than a simple statement of facts, I have drawn freely upon my imagination to reconstruct the conditions which likely prevailed at the first reading of Philippians. The facts are there and, I trust, are substantially correct, but they have been subordinated to the one purpose of getting the reader into a sympathetic frame of mind. Chapter 1 is an invitation to the reader to take his place among the Christians at Philippi to hear Paul's letter to them read for the first time."

The American Standard Version has been used throughout the book with the permission of the International Council of Religious Education, copyright holder.

In chapter 2 the translation used is Phillips' *Letters to Young Churches*. The translator expresses the hope that there will be times when the reader will completely forget that the words are a translation and feel their sense as if they were written for today.

### Suggestions for the Teacher

In presenting chapter 1 the teacher will seek to keep the vivid approach of the author in reconstructing the setting for the epistle. One way to do this is to let a good storyteller, well prepared in advance, narrate the story parts. These parts involve the material from the beginning of the chapter to the heading entitled "The Meeting Place," and the sections entitled "An Air of Expectancy," "The Mission of Epaphroditus," "Among Those Present," and "Reading the Letter."

It is suggested that the class teacher relate the sections entitled "The Meeting Place," "Across the Span of Troubled Years," and "The Church at Philippi."

All the material in these sections is based on research in conditions of that day and on a careful study of the book of Acts. The Scripture references in the footnotes are for the use of the teacher and other Bible students in verifying the author's statements.

The teacher should, by all means, plan the presentation of chapters 1 and 2 as a unit. Chapter 1 prepares for the reading aloud of Phillips' new translation of the epistle, provided in chapter 2. It should be read without discussion.

# Chapter I

# THE FIRST READING

The evening sun was glowing red above the hills of Macedonia as Prochorus, the freedman, moved about his self-assigned task of getting Lydia's compound ready for the believers who were to gather for worship there that night. There would be a larger attendance than usual that night in June, A. D. 62. In addition to placing the customary chairs, it was necessary to improvise some benches for those who were expected to fill the open courtyard at the appointed hour. Even with all Prochorus' preparations many would have to stand, because word had gotten out that Epaphroditus,[1] who had returned two days before from Rome, brought not only news fresh from Paul, but also a letter from him, written especially to the believers in Philippi.

The sight of so many extra seats gave to the place an atmosphere of expectancy. As he put all things in a final state of readiness for the meeting, the heart of Prochorus was full of deep satisfaction. Pouring oil into the lamps, he thought back across eighteen years to the time when he had come as a slave with Persis and his sister Lydia,[2] from Thyatira to open a market in Philippi for the sale of cloths dyed in the royal purple for which their city was famous. But the death of Persis shortly afterward had left the business in the hands of Lydia, whose intelligence and capacity for management were largely responsible for the success which had marked their enterprise from the first.

---

[1] Phil. 2:25.
[2] Acts 16:14.

[1]

The satisfaction, however, that welled up in the heart of Prochorus did not spring from the success of business. It came from the change Christ had wrought in his life and surroundings. Things had been different since that sabbath[3] afternoon nearly ten years ago when Lydia had returned from worshiping with a little group of Jewish women who customarily met for prayer by the Gangites River. A notable change had taken place in Lydia herself, even though this fine business woman was already known and respected for her ability and for the integrity of her personal life. A native of Asia, she had embraced the religion of the Jews, finding in Judaism the most satisfying answer to the hunger of her heart. And among these Jewish friends, who were a very small minority in the Roman colony of Philippi, she had won a place of high esteem for her devout life.

On that quiet Saturday afternoon four men had visited the little band of women worshipers. When the courtesy of addressing the group had been extended to the visitors, one of them, named Paul, acting as spokesman, had introduced his companions, Silas and a physician named Luke and a young attendant by the name of Timothy. With compelling earnestness Paul then told the story of Jesus, showing how the Jewish hope of a Messiah had been fulfilled by his death and resurrection.

As he was speaking, God opened Lydia's heart [4] to receive the message of salvation. Life had come where there had been only longing before, and everybody could see the difference in her. Not only was she herself subsequently baptized, but her household,[5] including Prochorus, followed her in an open profession of faith. A few weeks later at Lydia's insistence the four mission-

---

[3] Acts 16:13.
[4] Acts 16:14.
[5] Acts 16:15.

aries made their headquarters at her place of business.[6] Christianity had won its first foothold on the continent of Europe.

No special point had been made of it at the time, but as a perfectly natural outgrowth of the change that had taken place in Lydia, Prochorus was made a freedman. Somehow a new respect for the person and dignity of others had found its way into the company that sold the royal purple. Others of the household were given their freedom likewise; and now, sharing as partners in the business instead of as slaves, their renewed enthusiasm was reflected in an astonishing increase in the volume of business. Prochorus had every reason to sing for joy as he prepared for the gathering that night.

## I. THE MEETING PLACE

Lydia's establishment was admirably suited as a meeting place for the *hagioi,* or dedicated ones, as the church members called themselves. Her compound was located almost in the heart of the city of Philippi on a quiet street, only a few doors removed from its junction with the busy thoroughfare which ran past the forum. Ever since the Roman occupation of Macedonia, Philippi had ranked first [7] in importance in that district of the empire as both a military and a political center. Its citizens were proud of that fact; and though the city of Thessalonica, seventy miles westward, was larger in population and much more attractive commercially, Philippi basked in the prestige of its noble history and strategic importance. As a Roman colony [8] its life was patterned after that of Rome itself. Roman citizenship meant everything to

---

[6] Acts 16:15, 40.
[7] Acts 16:12.
[8] Acts 16:12.

one's standing, socially and otherwise, a fact which explains very largely why sales in purple, the official toga of Rome, supplied such a lucrative trade.

The shops where Lydia sold woven goods of all varieties extended along the front of the street. Well-stocked shelves served by attentive clerks conveyed the impression of thrift and business efficiency. Passing through the shops, however, one felt immediately the domestic atmosphere of a well-ordered home. The spacious courtyard, partly shaded by the overspreading branches of an oak, was completely enclosed by other buildings, which gave to the establishment an element of privacy.

Lydia and her household lived in the rooms across the back of the compound. The kitchen was conveniently located near a rear entrance and near the well, around which a small rock garden with carefully tended flowers bespoke a woman's love of things beautiful. Extending back along the left as one entered were other rooms—guestrooms, and an apartment occupied by Prochorus, the majordomo, and his family of three. On the opposite side the buildings were used very largely for storage purposes, but space had been provided also for classes during the day, where the *episkopoi,* or superintendents in charge of outstations, could come for study or could themselves conduct classes for inquirers and others interested in learning more of the Way.[9]

## II. An Air of Expectancy

But in the twilight of this lovely June evening as Prochorus prepared to light the lamps, the courtyard of Lydia resembled more a *theatron,* or meeting place for an audience of several hundred. By now the community

---

[9] Acts 24:14.

was accustomed to these gatherings at night on the first day of the week. In the lull of traffic on the busy thoroughfare near by, their pagan neighbors could often hear the voices of the *Christianoi* lifted in hymns [10] and spiritual songs as the worshipers made melody with their hearts unto their Lord.

Yes, it was just as Prochorus had surmised; tonight the attendance would be large. Already the *diakonoi,* men serving the church in the varied details of its effort to reach the needy with the gospel of love, were gathered in one of the spare rooms for reports of their activities and for prayer. Clement, who had been pastor of the church since the days when Paul and Timothy lived · among them, was standing at the main entrance to the courtyard with Lydia, their quiet conversation interrupted often by greetings to those who had come early. Some of these early arrivals were seated in silent prayer for the worship about to begin. Others were exchanging in quiet tones the word they had gathered from reported conversations with Epaphroditus and the latest news about Paul.

## III. ACROSS THE SPAN OF TROUBLED YEARS

It had been a long time since the believers at Philippi had heard anything directly from Paul. The last time they had seen him had been four years ago when he had taken his leave from them for Jerusalem.[11] Almost a year previously he had come to them unexpectedly from Ephesus by way of Troas, a couple of days' journey by ship across the Aegean Sea. Poor man! When they saw him then, his friends could scarcely hold back the

[10] Eph. 5:19.
[11] Acts 20:6.

tears, so sadly did his face reveal the effect of the awful ordeal through which he had just passed.[12]

Troubles rarely come singly, and Paul's case was no exception. Indeed, at that particular time when he had come from Asia, Satan had converged upon him from many directions as if to overwhelm him by the fury of his attacks. The great and effectual door which had opened to him in Ephesus [13] had been suddenly slammed shut in his face by the riot that terminated his three fruitful years in that stronghold of heathenism. There were enemies whose personal animosity found fuel for their hate among his critics at Corinth.[14] These had threatened to divide and destroy the work it had taken him so long to build in that strategic city. Things had seemed to be going to pieces all around him. The rift between Jewish Christians [15] and Gentile believers had been widening despite his best efforts. An extreme element among the Jewish Christians hotly resented receiving converts into church fellowship unless they first became Jews by submitting to the rite of circumcision.

These Judaizers, as they were called, had been forever on his trail, dogging his footsteps; like curs [16] they would never fight in the open but would yap at his heels every time his back was turned. On the other hand, some of the Gentile Christians had been slow about responding to Paul's effort to bridge the widening gap by gathering an offering for the poor among the *hagioi* at Jerusalem. That had been especially true at Corinth,[17] where there was much talk for two years, but little ac-

---

[12] Acts 20:1-2, but especially 2 Cor. 2:12-13.
[13] 1 Cor. 16:8 and Acts 20:1.
[14] 2 Cor. 11:13.
[15] Acts 15:1; 21:20; Gal. 2:4.
[16] Phil. 3:2.
[17] 2 Cor. 9:4-5.

tually done, about this project in which all the Gentile churches were united.

As a capstone to all his woes, sickness [18] had overtaken Paul. His old malady had returned, this time in a form so violent that even his beloved physician, Luke, despaired of his life. Writing from Philippi a month or two afterward, Paul had told the Corinthians of hearing the death sentence pronounced by these tragic circumstances.[19] But God, who raises the dead, had delivered him, and Paul had gone subsequently to Troas.[20] But when Titus had failed to meet him there with the expected word from Corinth, he had found no rest for his burdened spirit and had set out for Philippi, where he was sure of that kind of encouragement which only friends like those in that city could give.

After a ministry of less than a year with the churches of Macedonia and Achaia, Paul had left for Jerusalem,[21] with others appointed by the churches, to take their offering for the poor among the *hagioi* there. He had wanted, if possible, to arrive by the time of the feast of Pentecost,[22] only a few weeks away. Everyone in Philippi knew the tragic results of that trip to Jerusalem. The offering which had taken them so long to raise doubtless did some good, but it had failed to bridge [23] the growing chasm between the Jewish extremists and the Gentile believers. Paul's plan had backfired; instead of being healed, the breach had widened. Paul was mobbed and thrown into prison, where he waited two years for trial.[24]

---

[18] A. T. Robertson, *Epochs in the Life of Paul,* pp. 193-94.
[19] 2 Cor. 1:8-9.
[20] 2 Cor. 2:12-13.
[21] Acts 20:4-6.
[22] Acts 20:16.
[23] 2 Cor. 9:12-14.
[24] Acts 21:35-36; 24:27.

Afterward rumor had it that the apostle and his companions had been lost in a storm at sea while he was being transferred to Rome for trial there. But later it was learned that Paul had miraculously survived the storm and was kept in custody [25] at Rome awaiting a hearing before the emperor Nero. Since Julius,[26] the centurion in charge of Paul, was kindly disposed to his famous prisoner and since no one had been on hand to prefer any serious charge against him, Paul had been quartered in a house rented by the *Christianoi* at Rome, and was inconvenienced only by the presence of a guard, to whom he was chained by the wrist. Friends were allowed to come and go as they pleased. Life was not too hard, but there were long periods of deprivation because even the best of friends have a way of deferring the good which their hearts prompt them to do.

## IV. THE MISSION OF EPAPHRODITUS

The church at Philippi had hoped and prayed for Paul's speedy acquittal. They had longed to minister to his needs, but had lacked opportunity.[27] Besides, they had been expecting momentarily that some final disposition of his case would be made. As he was a Roman citizen, there was little danger that he would be thrown into the arena; but the stroke of execution fell often at the whim of the wicked Nero, and one could never tell what the outcome would be.

As the months of uncertainty passed, however, the *diakonoi* at Philippi had been finally stirred into action. One of their number, named Epaphroditus, volunteered to make the trip to Rome to visit Paul and bring back tidings. The church decided to defray his expenses and

---

[25] Acts 28:16, 30.
[26] Acts 27:1-3.
[27] Phil. 4:10.

make him a sort of ambassador of their love and good will. [28] He would not go empty-handed. Those things calculated to add to a man's comfort in prison would be sent along [29]—clothing, delicacies such as Paul loved to eat, letters from his many friends, and a generous gift of money which Epaphroditus would carefully sew in the belt which he wore next to his body. In all it had been quite a package which he had undertaken to carry on the two weeks' journey to the great city on the Tiber.

Again a long period of delay and uncertainty had distressed the friends at Philippi. Epaphroditus was due back; indeed, there had been time to make the trip over again and return, but still no word about him or his mission. Finally they had received the report that Epaphroditus after his arrival in Rome had fallen victim to the dread Roman fever, a disease which so often proved fatal. Another name had been added to the prayer list along with those of Paul and Timothy and Aristarchus [30] and others known to be at Rome.

And now, at long last, God, who answers the prayer of faith, had restored Epaphroditus to them again safe and sound, ready to tell his eager friends all about his adventure and the *Christianoi* in the thriving church at Rome.

## V. AMONG THOSE PRESENT

The crowd was gathering in greater numbers now. Watching their faces as they entered, Prochorus thought back to the beginnings of the gospel in Philippi ten years ago. It had been tough going for Paul from the first, even in that city which regarded itself as a model

---

[28] Phil. 2:25.
[29] Phil. 4:18.
[30] Col. 4:10.

of law and order. He remembered that Paul had once laughingly said the man from Macedonia whom he had seen in his vision at Troas [31] was certainly not standing with open arms to welcome his little party of missionaries when they arrived. It was a very small beginning which almost from the first had run into trouble.

Marcia could testify to that, thought Prochorus, as a young woman with the sweet face of a mystic entered to find her place in the gathering throng. Back in the clouded days of her life she had inadvertently brought trouble to Paul and Silas. At that time she was a slave who brought her masters a fortune by her soothsaying.[32] The demon who possessed her revealed with supernatural powers the answers which many troubled hearts sought: lost articles were found, missing loved ones located, business ventures sometimes forecast—all in such a way as to multiply the earnings of the wicked men who exploited her pathetic condition. But Paul had abruptly put an end to all of that when he addressed the demon in the power of the Name. With the overthrow of that evil dominion, trouble for the *Christianoi* had begun in real earnest. Her enraged masters had Paul and Silas publicly flogged and thrown into prison.[33]

Prochorus noted that the Philippian jailer also had joined the crowd that was gathering to hear from Paul. He seemed never to tire of telling how the apostle and his companion Silas had been delivered to him one day about dusk, their backs bleeding with the stripes applied by the Roman lictors.[34] A greater shake-up had taken place in him than the earthquake which rocked the city ten years ago. He had become a new creature [35] since

---

[31] Acts 16:9.
[32] Acts 16:16-18.
[33] Acts 16:19-22.
[34] Acts 16:23-34.
[35] 2 Cor. 5:17.

that night when he cried, "Sirs, what must I do to be saved?" To be sure, he kept his same position, but there was a new concern manifest for all who were committed to his keeping. Many of his prisoners had heard the story of Jesus, whose power to transform a life was so well illustrated in his own experience, and some had believed. Not a few of those present had been won to Christ by his consistent testimony through the years.

It was marvelous, Prochorus thought, how the good news had spread throughout that section to transform the lives of all who heeded its message of salvation in Jesus' name. Even some of the officials of the city had been enlisted. These men could never forget how Paul had commanded their respect of his rights as a Roman citizen. On the morning after the earthquake, when the magistrates had decided to drop the case which had been trumped up against the prisoners, Paul refused to let them take the easy way out.[36] His demand for a release befitting a Roman citizen who had been outraged by punishment before trial had made a lasting impression on them. Thus it happened that the personal force and magnetism of the man had won the hearts of some of these magistrates, along with the many slaves and aliens who now held citizenship in the kingdom of God.

But the reminiscent mood into which Prochorus had fallen was suddenly dispelled as Clement stood and formally called the meeting to order by announcing a hymn. He presided at such gatherings of the church and acted as a sort of shepherd to the flock, ministering to those in need and supervising in a general way the many activities sponsored by the church in the city. The reality of his Christian experience radiated from his face. There could be no doubt that his name was written in

---

[36] Acts 16:35-40.

heaven.[37] Prochorus had often thought that his name
had more than passing significance in relation to the
position he occupied in the church. *Clementus* was the
Latin adjective meaning kindly, benign. It seemed entirely fitting that by the providence of God a man with
such a name should be the leader in a church known
everywhere for its sweet reasonableness and the love
of its members one for another.

## VI. THE CHURCH AT PHILIPPI

That spirit of love was quite evident now in the way
they were singing and in the earnestness of their prayers.
Prochorus had not traveled extensively, but he had
worshiped on a number of occasions with the brethren at
Thessalonica and twice had spent some considerable time
at Corinth, where, of course, he worshiped with the
*hagioi* when they gathered on the Lord's Day. Although
his limited travels had not given him much opportunity
to judge among churches, Prochorus thought he knew
why Paul had such a warmth in his heart for the Philippians.

The Philippians were not as gifted as the church at
Corinth, nor as cultured, nor as rich in this world's
goods. In fact, except for Lydia and a relatively small
number who found steady employment with the Imperial
Government, they were downright poor.[38] Most of them
were slaves. The garments which they wore presented
visible proof of the low standard of living that prevailed
among them. But poverty was not the first impression
one gained from a visit with them, for they were rich
in the things that count—rich in their love, rich in their
discernment, rich in their readiness to respond to the

---

[37] Phil. 4:3.
[38] 2 Cor. 8:2.

opportunities of the gospel, rich in their loyalty [39] to the man whose labors among them had brought them true wealth of citizenship in God's eternal kingdom.

Repeatedly Paul had used them as an example to inspire [40] the liberality of others. In a letter to the Corinthians, written while among them, the great apostle had given the secret of this remarkable church. "First," he said, "they gave their own selves to the Lord, and to us through the will of God." [41] They had put first things first, and God had given them in return a foremost place for all time among those assemblies where the fellowship of kindred minds is like to that above. At least to Paul, whose travels had taken him through most of the Roman world, there was no church whose fellowship was so sweet and satisfying as that to be found among the *hagioi* at Philippi.

Even in Philippi, however, the ideal was only approached, never completely achieved. Satan's fierce opposition was abundantly attested, for false teachings sprang up like weeds and persecution was an ever-present threat. Some of the church had already triumphantly endured great suffering from this source, but others were yet to be tested.[42] There were also dissensions within. Of particular concern to all the spiritual-minded members of the church was the rift that had come about between two of their finest women, Euodia and Syntyche.[43] From the beginning, the progress of this unusual church had been in a large measure due to the active part taken by the women. It would be difficult to say whether their prominence in the work was due

---

[39] 2 Cor. 11:9; Phil. 4:15.
[40] 2 Cor. 8:1.
[41] 2 Cor. 8:5 ASV.
[42] Phil. 1:29.
[43] Phil. 4:2.

to the heritage of Greek culture which Macedonia enjoyed, or to the influence of Roman law, or simply to the circumstances in which the gospel took root.

But unfortunately strained feelings existed now between Euodia and Syntyche, who had figured so prominently in the successes of the past. On the surface it was nothing serious, only a matter of the administration of certain funds on which they could not see eye-to-eye, but disagreements over methods and procedures can stir up deep emotions and awaken resentments which destroy the teamwork that should prevail among God's children. Yet there was a more cheerful side. If it was not by accident that these two women were seated in different places in the assembly, it was also not by accident that both of them were there because they loved Paul dearly and would be listening carefully to every word from his pen. Both of them knew that the unity of the Spirit was the one thing above all that he desired among the followers of Christ.

## VII. READING THE LETTER

But now proceedings for that night reached the point' of chief interest. With fitting words of appreciation, Clement recognized Epaphroditus, who came forward to present the letter which Paul had sent by him to the church. This young *diakonos* still showed the effects of his recent illness and the strain of his two weeks' journey from Rome, but his face fairly glowed with the joy that this occasion afforded. Clement explained that after the reading of the letter by the clerk, Epaphroditus would relate his own experience and answer any questions about Paul and Timothy and the others at Rome.[44]

The letter itself, as the clerk carefully unrolled it, did

---

[44] See Eph. 6:21-22 for parallel case.

not appear long. It was neatly written in columns about three inches wide upon a sheet of papyrus about twenty inches in length and eight in width. The columns extended vertically across the eight inches, and the sheet was neatly rolled to facilitate handling and to preserve it from damage. Paul had used the everyday Greek, the world-speech at that time. He himself had written the salutation and the conclusion to authenticate the letter as his,[45] but the substance of his message, which covered both sides of the sheet of papyrus, was written in the neat script of an amanuensis, or stenographer especially trained for the task.[46] Such was Paul's custom with the letters for which he was already famous, letters which were carefully treasured by the churches that received them.

Prochorus observed to himself that there was something about Paul's letters that made them different. This one he was about to hear, for instance, would certainly deal in a most natural way with matters of personal interest between its writer and those who had gathered to hear it read. Clearly the immediate occasion of Paul's writing had been the fact that Epaphroditus was returning from Rome. He was the most appropriate messenger by whom to acknowledge receipt of their timely gift and to express thanks for their generosity. But along with this there would certainly be an unfolding of revealed truth which had been in a peculiar way committed to the apostle by the Lord Jesus himself. When Paul wrote, it was as though God himself had breathed into the everyday experiences and problems with which he dealt the solution of eternal, life-giving principles. Invariably there was more to his letters than could be grasped at a first reading. Pastors and teachers would

---

[45] 2 Thess. 3:17. See also Gal. 6:11.
[46] Rom. 16:22.

unfold lesson after lesson of quickening truth as they studied and applied the teaching in each of them.

It had been that way with copies of letters written to other churches, and Prochorus felt sure that it would be that way with this letter to the Philippians, which he was about to hear read for the first time. Copies of it would be carefully made and circulated among the church members there, and sent to believers in other places as well.[47] Prochorus was glad that in this manner the word of salvation would be circulated in spite of fetters and prison cells.

Could he have looked across the centuries to see the great host of believers who are undertaking this study of its contents, his joy would have exceeded all bounds.

### QUESTIONS FOR REVIEW AND EXAMINATION

1. Read Acts 16:14-40 and find who were the first members of the church at Philippi.
2. What facts are given us about Epaphroditus in Philippians 2:25-30; 4:18; and 4:21-22?

---

[47] Col. 4:16.

# CHAPTER II

# THE LETTER TO THE CHRISTIANS
# AT PHILIPPI [1]

NOTE—It is suggested that this translation of Paul's letter to the Philippians be read aloud to the class in the lesson immediately following the study of the previous chapter. A good reader, carefully enlisted in ample time to acquaint himself with the text, will greatly enhance the desired effect.

Paul and Timothy, true servants of Jesus Christ, to the bishops, deacons and all true Christians at Philippi, grace and peace from God the Father and Jesus Christ the Lord!

### I HAVE THE MOST PLEASANT MEMORIES OF YOU ALL

I thank God for you Christians at Philippi whenever I think of you. My constant prayers for you are a real joy, for they bring back to my mind how we have worked together for the Gospel from the first. I feel sure that the One who has begun His good work in you will go on developing it until the Day of Jesus Christ. It is only natural that I should feel like this about you all, for during the time I was in prison as well as when I was out defending and demonstrating the power of the Gospel we shared together the grace of God. God knows how much I long, with the deepest Christian love and affection, for your companionship. My prayer for you is that you may have still more love—a love that is full of knowledge and wise insight. I want you to be able always to recognize the highest and the best, and to live sincere and blameless lives until the Day of Jesus Christ. I want to

---

[1] J. B. Phillips, *Letters to Young Churches.* New York: The Macmillan Company. 1947. Used by permission.

[17]

see your lives full of true goodness, produced by the power that Jesus Christ gives you to the praise and glory of God.

## MY IMPRISONMENT HAS TURNED OUT TO BE NO BAD THING

Now, concerning myself, I want you to know, my brothers, that what has happened to me has, in effect, turned out to the advantage of the Gospel. For, first of all, my imprisonment means a personal witness for Christ before the Palace guards, not to mention others who come and go. Then, it means that most of our brothers, somehow taking fresh heart in the Lord from the very fact that I am a prisoner for Christ's sake, have shown far more courage in boldly proclaiming the word of God. I know that some are preaching Christ out of jealousy, in order to annoy me, but some are preaching Him in good faith. The motive of the former is questionable —they preach in a partisan spirit, hoping to make my chains even more galling than they would otherwise be. But what does it matter? However they may look at it, the fact remains that Christ *is* being preached, whether sincerely or not, and that fact makes me very happy. Yes, and I shall go on being very happy, for I know that what is happening will be for the good of my own soul, thanks to your prayers and the resources of the Spirit of Jesus Christ. It all accords with my own earnest wishes and hopes, which are that I should never be in any way ashamed, but that now, as always, I should honour Christ with the utmost boldness by the way I live, whether that means I am to face death or to go on living. For living to me means simply "Christ," and if I die I should merely gain more of Him. I realise, of course, that the work which I have started may make it necessary for me to go on living in this world. I should find it very hard to make a choice. I am torn in two directions— on the one hand I long to leave this world and live with Christ, and that is obviously the best thing for me. Yet, on the other hand, it is probably more necessary for you that

I should stay here on earth. That is why I feel pretty well convinced that I shall not leave this world yet, but shall be able to stand by you, to help you forward in Christian living and to find increasing joy in your faith. So you can look forward to making much of me as your minister in Christ when I come to see you again!

But whatever happens, make sure that your everyday life is worthy of the Gospel of Christ. So that whether I do come and see you, or merely hear about you from a distance, I may know that you are standing fast in a united spirit, battling with a single mind for the faith of the Gospel and not caring two straws for your enemies. The very fact that they are your enemies is plain proof that they are lost to God, while the fact that you have such men as enemies is plain proof that you yourselves are being saved by God. You are given, in this battle, the privilege not merely of believing in Christ but also of suffering for His sake. It is now your turn to take part in that battle you once saw me engaged in, and which, in point of fact, I am still fighting.

### ABOVE ALL THINGS BE LOVING, HUMBLE, UNITED

Now if your experience of Christ's encouragement and love means anything to you, if you have known something of the fellowship of His Spirit, and all that it means in kindness and deep sympathy, do make my best hopes for you come true! Live together in harmony, live together in love, as though you had only one mind and one spirit between you. Never act from motives of rivalry or personal vanity, but in humility think more of each other than you do of yourselves. None of you should think only of his own affairs, but should learn to see things from other people's point of view.

### LET CHRIST BE YOUR EXAMPLE OF HUMILITY

Let Christ Himself be your example as to what your attitude should be. For He, who had always been God by nature, did not cling to His prerogatives as God's Equal, but stripped Himself of all privilege by consenting to be a slave by nature and being born as a mortal man. And, having become man, He humbled Himself by living a life of utter obedience, even to the extent of dying, *and the death he died was the death of a common criminal.* That is why God has now lifted Him so high, and has given Him the Name beyond all names, so that at the Name of Jesus "every knee shall bow," whether in Heaven or Earth or under the earth. And that is why, in the end, "every tongue shall confess" that Jesus Christ is the Lord, to the glory of God the Father.

### GOD IS HIMSELF AT WORK WITHIN YOU

So then, my dearest friends, as you have always followed my advice—and that not only when I was present to give it— so now that I am far away be keener than ever to work out the salvation that God has given you with a proper sense of awe and responsibility. For it is God Who is at work within you, giving you the will and the power to achieve His purpose.

Do all you have to do without grumbling or arguing, so that you may be God's children, blameless, sincere and wholesome, living in a warped and diseased world, and shining there like lights in a dark place. For you hold in your hands the very word of life. Thus can you give me something to be proud of in the day of Christ, for I shall know then that I did not spend my energy in vain. Yes, and if it should happen that my life-blood is, so to speak, poured out upon the sacrifice and offering which your faith means to God, then I can still be very happy, and I can share my happiness with you all. I should like to feel that you could be glad about this too, and could share with me the happiness I speak of.

## I AM SENDING EPAPHRODITUS WITH
## THIS LETTER, AND TIMOTHY LATER

But I hope in Jesus Christ that it will not be long before I can send Timothy to you, and then I shall be cheered by a first-hand account of you and your doings. I have nobody else with a genuine interest in your well-being. All the others seem to be wrapped up in their own affairs and do not really care for the business of Jesus Christ. But you know how Timothy has proved his worth, working with me for the Gospel like a son with his father. I hope to send him to you as soon as I can tell how things will work out for me, but God gives me some hope that it will not be long before I am able to come myself as well. I have considered it desirable, however, to send you Epaphroditus. He has been to me brother, fellow-worker and comrade-in-arms, as well as being the messenger you sent to see to my wants. He has been home-sick for you, and was worried because he knew that you had heard that he was ill. Indeed he was ill, very dangerously ill, but God had mercy on him—and incidentally on me as well, so that I did not have the sorrow of losing him to add to my sufferings. I am particularly anxious, therefore, to send him to you so that when you see him again you may be glad, and to know of your joy will lighten my own sorrows. Welcome him in the Lord with great joy! You should hold men like him in highest honour, for his loyalty to Christ brought him very near death—he risked his life to do for me in person what distance prevented you all from doing.

In conclusion, my brothers, delight yourselves in the Lord! It doesn't bore me to repeat a piece of advice like this, and if you follow it you will find it a great safeguard to your souls.

### THE "CIRCUMCISION" PARTY ARE THE
### ENEMIES OF YOUR FAITH AND FREEDOM

Be on your guard against these curs, these wicked work-
men, these would-be mutilators of your bodies! We are,
remember, truly circumcised when we worship God by the
Spirit, when we find our joy in Christ Jesus and put no confidence in what we are in the flesh.

### I WAS EVEN MORE OF A JEW THAN THESE JEWS,
### YET KNOWING CHRIST HAS CHANGED
### MY WHOLE LIFE

If it were right to have such confidence, I could certainly
have it, and if any of these men thinks he has grounds for
such confidence I can assure him I have more. I was born
a true Jew, I was circumcised on the eighth day, I was a
member of the tribe of Benjamin, I was in fact a full-blooded
Jew. As far as keeping the Law is concerned I was a Pharisee,
and you can judge my enthusiasm for the Jewish faith by my
active persecution of the Church. As far as the Law's
righteousness is concerned, I don't think anyone could have
found fault with me. Yet every advantage that I had gained
I considered lost for Christ's sake. Yes, and I look upon
everything as loss compared with the overwhelming gain
of knowing Christ Jesus my Lord. For His sake I did in
actual fact suffer the loss of everything, but I considered it
useless rubbish compared with being able to win Christ.
For now my place is in Him, and I am not dependent upon
any of the self-achieved righteousness of the Law. God has
given me that genuine righteousness which comes from faith
in Christ. How changed are my ambitions! Now I long to
know Christ and the power shown by His Resurrection: now
I long to share His sufferings, even to die as He died, so
that I may perhaps attain, as He did, the resurrection from
the dead. Yet, my brothers, I do not consider myself to have

"arrived," spiritually, nor do I consider myself already perfect. But I keep going on, grasping ever more firmly that purpose for which Christ grasped me. My brothers, I do not consider myself to have fully grasped it even now. But I do concentrate on this: I leave the past behind and with hands outstretched to whatever lies ahead I go straight for the goal—my reward the honour of being called by God in Christ.

### MY AMBITION IS THE TRUE GOAL OF THE
### SPIRITUALLY ADULT: MAKE IT YOURS TOO

All of us who are spiritually adult should set ourselves this sort of ambition, and if at present you cannot see this, yet you will find that this is the attitude which God is leading you to adopt. It is important that we go forward in the light of such truth as we have ourselves attained to.

Let me be your example here, my brothers: let my example be the standard by which you can tell who are the genuine Christians among those about you. For there are many, of whom I have told you before and tell you again now, even with tears, that they are the enemies of the Cross of Christ. These men are heading for utter destruction—their god is their own appetite, their pride is in what they should be ashamed of, and this world is the limit of their horizon. But we are citizens of Heaven; our outlook goes beyond this world to the hopeful expectation of the Saviour Who will come from Heaven, the Lord Jesus Christ. He will re-make these wretched bodies of ours to resemble His own glorious Body, by that power of His which makes Him the Master of everything that is.

So, my brothers whom I love and long for, my joy and my crown, do stand firmly in the Lord, and remember how much I love you.

### BE UNITED: BE JOYFUL: BE AT PEACE

Euodias and Syntyche, I beg you by name to make up your differences as Christians should! And you, my true fellow-worker, I ask you to help these women. They both worked hard with me for the Gospel, as did Clement and all my other fellow-workers whose names are in the Book of Life.

Delight yourselves in God, yes, find your joy in Him at all times. Have a reputation for gentleness, and never forget the nearness of your Lord.

Don't worry over anything whatever; tell God every detail of your needs in earnest and thankful prayer, and the peace of God, which transcends human understanding, will keep constant guard over your hearts and minds as they rest in Christ Jesus.

Here is a last piece of advice. If you believe in goodness and if you value the approval of God, fix your minds on the things which are holy and right and pure and beautiful and good. Model your conduct on what you have learned from me, on what I have told you and shown you, and you will find that the God of peace will be with you.

### THE MEMORY OF YOUR GENEROSITY IS
#### AN ABIDING JOY TO ME

It has been a great joy to me that after all this time you have shown such interest in my welfare. I don't mean that you had forgotten me, but up till now you had no opportunity of expressing your concern. Nor do I mean that I have been in actual need, for I have learned to be content, whatever the circumstances may be. I know now how to live when things are difficult and I know how to live when things are prosperous. In general and in particular I have learned the secret of facing either poverty or plenty. I am ready for anything through the strength of the One Who lives within me. Nevertheless I am not disparaging the way in which you were willing to share my troubles. You Philippians will remember that in the early days of the gospel when I left Macedonia, you were the only church who shared with me the fellowship of giving and receiving. Even in Thessalonica you twice sent me help when I was in need. It isn't the value of the gift that I am keen on, it is the reward that will come to you because of these gifts that you have made.

Now I have everything I want—in fact I am rich. Yes, I am quite content, thanks to your gifts received through Epaphroditus. Your generosity is like a lovely fragrance, a sacrifice that pleases the very heart of God. My God will supply all that you need from His glorious resources in Christ Jesus. And may glory be to our God and our Father for ever and ever, Amen!

### FAREWELL MESSAGES

Greetings to every true Christian, from me and all the brothers here with me. All the Christians here would like to send their best wishes, particularly those who belong to the Emperor's household.

The grace of the Lord Jesus Christ be with your spirit.

PAUL.

### QUESTIONS FOR REVIEW AND EXAMINATION

1. Does the book of Philippians seem to indicate that Paul felt a special love for these people? Select some of the clearest statements of his love, and give the references from your Bible. (You may consider Phil. 1:3, 7-8; 2:19, 24; 4:1.)

2. Indicate your favorite section of Philippians and tell why you have chosen it.

# CHAPTER III
# POINT OF VIEW AND OUTLINE

One of the best approaches in studying any book of the Bible is to get a bird's-eye view of it in its entirety. Only after seeing it thus can the student fully appreciate the particular message of each paragraph or verse. With the reading of this lovely letter still fresh in mind, let us now examine the book of Philippians more carefully as a unit. It is hoped that through such an approach each part will yield its truest message and contribute to the general effect of the whole study.

An able Bible teacher once likened this procedure to that of a traveler visiting a famous city for the first time. Instead of going directly to one point of interest after another, the experienced tourist will first get a bird's-eye view of the city itself from some place of advantage. Then, with the general layout of the city in mind and his own sense of direction firmly established, he will proceed to explore it street by street, spending as long as he might wish at the several places of interest.

Books of the Bible are like cities in this respect. They have their main streets, their points of renown, and their residential districts where kindred ideas live. Having seen the whole, one may follow the main thoroughfare and take a quick look around, or he may proceed more leisurely, verse by verse. In either case the impressions from his visit will be more satisfactory for his having taken the time to relate each part to the whole.

Finding the vantage point from which to make such a survey is a matter of utmost importance. It involves, first of all, a humble attitude of the heart, a willingness to obey the truth as God reveals it, for we are not idle sightseers in the pages of the New Testament. In the next place it involves an attentive mind, a willingness to do some mental climbing. The first step is subjective, and challenges the sincerity of our purpose in any study of the Scriptures. The second step is objective, and challenges us to find that statement of truth from which the entire epistle may be seen in its true proportions, the verse which will prove the master key to all its treasuries of truth.

## I. OUR PERSONAL ATTITUDE AND GOD'S REVEALED TRUTH

What a man sees depends primarily on where he is. That statement sounds like a truism; yet many people ignore it completely in their quest for spiritual truth. We must bear in mind that we are seeking God's revelation in the Philippian epistle. To find that revelation is more than an intellectual process. It is an experience made possible only as the eyes of the heart are enlightened by the Holy Spirit and the truth revealed is received in the obedience of faith.

This personal aspect of our Bible study has always been God's chief concern. His very first question to Adam after the tragedy of sin was, "Where art thou?" (Gen. 3:9 ASV). And today, every time we undertake to study the Bible, we may be sure that God still wants us to know where we ourselves stand in relation to the truth that he longs to disclose. Are we willing to accept the white light of the truth which this epistle will throw upon our own lives?

When people complain that they cannot catch the message or see the beauty in a certain passage of the Bible, their difficulty is not always one of intellect. More than likely an unwillingness to follow the light they have already received accounts for their failure to enjoy the delights of a fuller revelation. For example, how can anyone who has not endured hardship for the gospel of Jesus Christ get much out of Philippians, unless he becomes willing to endure that hardship for Christ's sake? How can he whose heart has not been prepared by fellowship in the sufferings it describes know the joy of which it speaks?

## II. Seeking the Artist's Perspective

In studying a masterpiece the visitor will want to look at it from many different angles and under different lighting effects. In each case some new feature, some fresh tone or color, will become apparent. In a very real way, however, the artist himself determines the point of view by the picture he paints. The perspective is of his own making, and if one is to see the picture at its best, it must be hung at the height and under the lighting effect dictated by his brush.

This necessity of finding the artist's own perspective was strikingly impressed upon the writer in an experience with Raphael's great painting, *The Transfiguration*, which hangs on the walls of the Vatican Gallery in Rome. There the famous artist gives his conception of the scene that took place on the mountaintop as Jesus was transfigured before the eyes of his wondering disciples. On the same canvas Raphael portrays a contrasting scene, the event that was transpiring at the foot of the mountain. The perplexity of the disciples and the distress of the father who had brought his afflicted son to them for healing are presented in sharp contrast to the majesty in the scene above.

To the writer, however, this picture had always seemed out of proportion, as though the artist, in an almost grotesque attempt, were crowding scenes too widely removed upon the same canvas. The same feeling came upon him as he stood one day before the original. Disturbed by this impression, he walked out of the room into another where the guide abruptly stopped him. "This is the place," he said, "from which to see *The Transfiguration*." Turning, he saw Raphael's masterpiece framed by the doorway through which he had just passed. The crowded effect was gone. In the transfigured Son of God, majestic sweetness hovered low over the tragedy of human need and human failure. The visitor had found the artist's perspective and was awed by the sublimity of God's nearness to man. Even so, the author of a book will determine the point of view from which we may best study it.

Of course, the book of Philippians, like any other real work of art, can be seen with profit from many different points of view. In each case some new feature of the artist's message will become evident. This is always true of the Bible and of any book in it. In shadow or in sunshine, at any stage in life's pilgrimage, one may turn to it assured of catching fresh meaning in its familiar truths. But our best view of the book will appear if we can find the key verse—that statement in the epistle which yields Paul's own position as he wrote it—for from that point of view alone can the epistle be seen to the best advantage.

### III. "This Is the Place"

What, then, is the artist's perspective as determined by the Philippian letter itself? From what place can we best see its picture of revealed truth? Granting to each student the right to answer that question for himself, your guide in this chapter would conduct his party unhesitatingly to Paul's classic statement, "For to me to live is Christ" (Phil. 1:21 ASV). It can all be summed up, so far as Paul is concerned, in: "To live is Christ." But simply to cite this verse is not enough. One is not suddenly transported to this vantage point by the magic of a word. He cannot really take this position until he understands the meaning of the phrase in terms of his own experience and is thus able to appreciate for himself the approach which it affords. Such an understanding will require considerable effort, but if one can see this letter as related to the other letters written by Paul, especially those of the imprisonment, it will be worth all the effort it costs.

## IV. PHILIPPIANS AND THE OTHER LETTERS OF THE IMPRISONMENT

Paul's letter to the Philippians was one of four epistles written about the same time, while he was a prisoner in Rome. The others are Philemon, Colossians, and Ephesians. Philemon is a very personal letter written to a Christian by that name about a runaway slave who had been won to Christ by Paul.

The letter addressed to the church at Colosse—a city which incidentally Paul himself had never visited—is concerned chiefly with the person of Christ. In reply to some false teachers (Gnostics) who were trying to represent Jesus as the last in a long series of emanations from a God who was too pure and exalted to be contaminated by such close association with flesh and blood, Paul presents Christ as pre-eminent above all.

Ephesians seems to have been a circular letter to all the churches in the vicinity of Ephesus. In many respects it is the profoundest message ever penned, disclosing the glory of Christ's person, the grandeur of God's plan for the ages, and the mystery of grace whereby believers are made one body with Christ, sharing even here and now his life in the heavenlies.

There are three other groups of letters written by Paul,[1] and each group, having a common bond in point of circumstance, makes its own peculiar emphasis. The substance of the revealed truth of the gospel is, of course, the same in all of them, but different aspects of that truth are developed according to the inner growth and outer circumstances of the writer. For this reason a familiarity with the other letters in a group makes for a truer appreciation of any one of them.

Colossians and especially Ephesians will help in understanding Philippians. Their common bonds are Paul's extended imprisonment of nearly four years and the Gnostic heresy which was beginning to cast its threat over the churches Paul had founded in Asia Minor.

## 1. *The Pre-eminence of Christ*

The Gnostic heresy was a direct challenge to the person and dignity of Christ. It sprang from a sort of dualism which held matter to be evil in itself and thus forever separated from spirit, which is good. In order to bridge this gulf, it was argued that Christ was the last in a series of eons, or emanations from God to man—a sort of demigod taking his rank with others in the line of celestial authority.[2]

---

[1] These groups, for convenience, may be listed as: the missionary letters—1 and 2 Thessalonians; the doctrinal letters—1 and 2 Corinthians, Galatians, and Romans; and the pastoral letters—1 and 2 Timothy and Titus.

[2] It would appear that Paul's exaltation of Christ in answer to the challenge of this heresy has received better treatment at the hands of commentators than his answer to the challenge of four long years of imprisonment. Perhaps that is because the former is more apparent and can be dealt with more objectively.

We find Paul answering this false teaching in each of the three epistles of this group. We shall see in Philippians 2:6-9 that the preincarnate Christ existed from the beginning on an equality with God and for the things which he suffered has been given the "name which is above every name." In the opening verses of Ephesians the Father's choice in Christ was "before the foundation of the world," and it is his good pleasure "to sum up all things in Christ, the things in the heavens, and the things upon the earth" (Eph. 1:4, 10 ASV). His partaking of flesh and blood and the suffering of death, so far from being an indication of inferiority in rank, is an occasion for renewed exaltation. God "raised him from the dead, and made him to sit at his right hand in the heavenly places, far above all rule, and authority, and power, and dominion, and every name that is named, not only in this world, but also in that which is to come" (vv. 20-21 ASV).

As might be expected from a letter written to a church in the deepest shadow of this false teaching, Colossians comes directly to the same point. Christ, "the Son of his love . . . is the image of the invisible God, the first-born of all creation; for in him were all things created, in the heavens and upon the earth, things visible and things invisible, whether thrones or dominions or principalities or powers; all things have been created through him, and unto him; and he is before all things, and in him all things consist" (Col. 1:13-17 ASV).

## 2. *Comfort and Courage from Our Oneness with Him*

All these passages take on fresh meaning in the light of the controversy then current about the position of Christ. The point that may be overlooked, however, is their meaning in the light of Paul's four years of heartache, loneliness, and disappointment behind prison walls.

What does Christ's place of pre-eminence mean to the prisoner of Christ and to other believers who share with him the hardships of the prison cell? What does it mean to us today who are continually faced with failure and frustration?

To Paul, the revelation of God's grace in answer to these sufferings was unspeakably glorious. *The prisoner in captivity was one with the Prince in glory. Their life was one—in quality, in destiny, and in present victory despite apparent defeat.*

For this reason emphasis in these letters of the imprisonment falls, not only upon the exaltation of Christ, but also upon the believer's oneness with him. Especially is this true of Ephesians. Here part of our difficulty in understanding Paul's teachings concerning the church as the body of Christ grows out of our reluctance to recognize the oneness of our life with his. The union is so complete as to require the idea of corporate identity for its logical expression.

The oneness of believers with their Lord, therefore, is the oneness of the body with its head. This is an old figure with Paul (1 Cor. 12 and Rom. 12:4-8), but its application now extends far beyond the functional problems of a local church. The privilege of such a oneness is to the fore. Its disclosure was part of the "unsearchable riches of Christ" (Eph. 3:8 ASV). Through this gospel even the heathen may now become "fellow-heirs, and fellow-members of the body, and fellow-partakers of the promise in Christ Jesus" (Eph. 3:6 ASV).

If Christ, having been raised from the dead, is made to sit at the Father's right hand "in heavenly places, far above all rule, and authority, and power, and dominion, and every name that is named" (Eph. 1:20-21), he occupies that place for the advantage of his body—for all who are joined to him in the living union of faith. It was given him to be "head over all things to [the advantage of] the church, which is his body, the fulness of him that filleth all in all" (vv. 22-23 ASV). In fact the very power which raised him up is operative now in its "exceeding greatness" toward us who believe (v. 19).[3]

According to the Scriptures "we died with Christ" (Rom. 6:8 ASV); we were "buried with him" (Col. 2:12 ASV); we were "made . . . alive together with Christ . . . , and raised . . . up with him, and made . . . to sit with him in heavenly places" (Eph. 2:5-6 ASV). There is a five-fold "togetherness." The identity is complete; our lives are one with his life. All this Paul packs into his statement, "For to me to live is Christ."

At this point the reader is probably wondering why so much is being said about Ephesians in a book purporting to be written about Philippians. The reason is this: The letter to the Philippians is a practical demonstration of the truth in Ephesians. The oneness of our life with Christ's is disclosed in Ephesians, but in Philippians we see what that kind of life means to a man living in a prison under the shadow of the headsman's ax. The pattern of the Ephesian epistle, so aptly described by

---

[3] With so much said about the exaltation of Jesus, it is not surprising that in Ephesians also, more clearly than anywhere else, we are given the doctrinal significance of the ascension.

"When he ascended on high, he led captivity captive,
And gave gifts to men" (Eph. 4:8).

By his incarnation the Son of God entered the life-stream of the human race. There, as a man, he translated God's quality of life into human experience. In him eternal life found human expression. When Jesus ascended, he took with him something that had never been in heaven before. He carried this human expression of the divine nature as a trophy back to the Father's right hand, whence it could be communicated by his indwelling Spirit to all who believe. That is how the believer shares in the life of the Son of God.

Dr. W. O. Carver in the title of his book as *The Glory of God in the Christian Calling,* must be woven into the texture of human experience. Philippians is of the cloth which comes from such a loom. One must have a familiarity with Ephesians to understand Philippians for the same reason that one must know the principles of physics to understand what is taking place in the laboratory. Philippians glows with the radiance of the Christ-life, touching and transfiguring the troubled ways of man.

### 3. *Christ, Our Life*

Christ is our life, as well as Paul's. What he says of himself he applies to others who believe with him. "For ye died, and your life is hid with Christ in God. When Christ, who is our life [many ancient authorities read "your" life], shall be manifested, then shall ye also with him be manifested in glory" (Col. 3:3-4 ASV). This quality of life bears unmistakably the stamp of the resurrection and for that reason can be communicated only to that which has died. All of this, of course, is set forth in the beautiful symbolism of baptism, which we Baptists have zealously guarded, especially with reference as to the form and the authority of its administration. But the quality of our living would indicate that many have failed to grasp God's emphasis on the source and the nature of the "newness of life" depicted in the ordinance.

One does not live Christ as a baseball fan lives baseball or as a salesman "sold on his line" eats, drinks and talks his sales. Rather, one lives Christ as the branch lives the vine that bears it. The flow of life is the same. The well-being, the fruitfulness, of the branch is one and the same with that of the vine and of all the other branches as well (John 15:1-8). This is true of any organism, whether the figure God uses be that of vine or body.

The oneness of the branch with the vine helps us to understand what Paul means when he says, "For me to live is Christ." The fruit to which he refers in Philippians 1:11, "being filled with the fruit of righteousness," is one and the same with that described in Galatians 5:22 as "the fruit of the Spirit." There are nine words which describe the nature of that fruit. "But the fruit of the Spirit is love, joy, peace, longsuffering, kindness, goodness, faithfulness, meekness, self-control" (ASV). The first luscious grapes to ripen in this cluster are love, joy, and peace. These are inner characteristics. In other words, God seems to be saying, "If you go in seriously for living this life of the Spirit, you will be the very first one to enjoy its fruit. 'The husbandman that laboreth must [naturally] be the first to partake of the fruits' [2 Tim. 2:6]. Before others are aware of your longsuffering, kindness, goodness, and all the rest of it, your own heart will sing with love, joy and peace."

## V. THE OUTLINE TAKES SHAPE

For Paul, Philippians is that song. Thus it is not by accident or by any artificial imposition of one verse upon others that this phrase, "love, joy, peace," becomes the outline for the epistle. The words form a convenient mental hat rack, to be sure, upon which the development of thought in the letter may be hung, but the right to use them thus stems from the nature of the life reflected in the book itself. When seen from the viewpoint of one who can say, "For me to live is Christ," Philippians unfolds as the epistle of love, joy, and peace.

For convenience' sake Philippians 1:1-11 may be designated as the *love section*. Philippians 1:12 to 3:21 may be designated as the *joy section*. Joy is the dominant note. The sparkling waters in Paul's reservoir of joy are fed like a mountain lake from two main sources high up in the snowcapped heavenlies. One of these sources (1:12-30 to 2:30) may be described as the thrill of continuous triumph known only to those whose lives are completely identified with the fortunes of the gospel. The exultation of being more than conquerors makes of trial and sufferings an unspeakable privilege. The other source (3:1-21) may be described as the thrill of possessing life's greatest treasure, of gaining Christ, who revises all standards of values because he is the pearl of great price. There are, of course, other tributaries which we shall explore together.

Philippians 4:1-23 may be designated as the *peace section*. There the flood tides of God's great peace come in to bear us up above the miseries of life's shoals and shallows. Christians are to be at peace among themselves (vv. 1-3), and within themselves (vv. 5-9), and with the surroundings in which their lot is cast (vv. 10-23).

But the point for emphasis as one views this lovely panorama, is that love, joy, and peace are not ends to be sought in themselves. They are by-products. What must be sought above all else is that Life which yields such fruitage.

## To Live Is Christ

For me to live is Christ!—This is the key
To life, through death of all of self and sin;
The golden Door where I may enter in;
The Blood-stained passport of my liberty.

For me, to live is Christ!—Wrapped in His love,
To know His fellowship of suffering—to take
With Him the Calvary road for others' sakes;
Yet see the glory shining from above.

For me to live, is Christ!—Oh, matchless flow,
Current of Life eternal and divine!
What floods of holy ecstasy are mine!
What joy the soul thus sanctified may know!

O wond'rous Saviour, peerless Sacrifice;
Forevermore, for me to live is Christ!

A. M. QUICK [4]

## QUESTIONS FOR REVIEW AND EXAMINATION

1. What principles of effective Bible study does this chapter bring out in regard to:
    The value of seeing a book as a whole?
    The way one's own attitude affects his understanding?
    The need to discover the author's point of view?
    What is suggested as the key verse for Philippians?

2. What is the predominant teaching about Jesus Christ in Ephesians, Colossians, and Philippians? How does Paul use this truth to refute a false doctrine? What joy and comfort did this truth about Christ give him in prison?

3. Into what three sections may Philippians be divided?

[4] From A Gospel Courier. Milwaukee: Herald of Holiness, publisher. Used by permission.

# CHAPTER IV
# WHERE LOVE ABOUNDS

## PHILIPPIANS 1:1-11

One does not read far into the letter of Philippians before becoming aware of the atmosphere of love in which it was written. The first eleven verses with which this chapter deals are characterized by a spirit of loving confidence. They are joyous and gladsome, radiant with the light of heaven. Their tone is assured, inspiring confidence; their appeal is warm and tender with a love that overflows in prayer. The Christian fellowship which they reveal is at the highest level, strengthened rather than strained by the miles and months that separated the writer from his readers.

Spiritual growth and fruitfulness are more a matter of atmosphere than many of us realize. Each one has a responsibility in creating the necessary conditions of love and confidence in which all may come into Christian maturity. It is hoped that a study of this letter will do much toward fostering such an atmosphere in all our churches and denominational gatherings. This would seem a worthy purpose to which we might well dedicate ourselves as we pray and walk together through these pages.

## I. CHRISTIAN GREETINGS (vv. 1-2)

In the opening salutation our attention is directed to the sender, the recipients, and the nature of the greeting itself.

The form for letters varies among different people and in different ages. There is much to commend the style

[39]

that was in effect when Paul wrote the Philippians. The sender's name appeared first instead of last as is the custom with us. This saved the reader the trouble of looking to the end of a letter to see by whom it was written. Paul begins with his own name and includes Timothy with himself. This does not mean, of course, that Timothy was joint author. It is characteristic of Paul's way of identifying himself with his colleagues in the work. The success of his labors lay to no small degree in his ability to enlist others. The church in Philippi would bear the young assistant, Timothy, in grateful remembrance and would be better prepared by this inclusion to receive him when he should come on his next mission (Phil. 2:19).

Paul calls himself and Timothy "slaves of Christ Jesus." It is one of his favorite designations. There was no occasion for him to use his official title of "apostle" as there was in his letters to the churches of Galatia and Corinth, where some opponents challenged his authority. Among those who knew him best and loved him most he was simply a slave of Christ Jesus. That term may not be so readily appreciated today as it was a hundred years ago. A type of slavery still exists, but its form has changed. We may thank God that men and women no longer are sold like cattle. But Paul saw in the figure of a bond slave his own position in relation to Christ, and gloried in it. The term he applied to himself, he urged also upon us. "Ye are not your own; for ye were bought with a price" (1 Cor. 6:19 ASV).

The Philippian Christians are addressed as "saints." The blood of Jesus which was the price of their redemption was upon them and marked them as holy. Paul was especially fond of the word and often addressed the believers as "saints" to remind them of the sacred nature of this purchase and to challenge them with its noble purpose. But these saints wore no halos as they walked the streets of Philippi. They were men and women of flesh and blood, of like passions with ourselves and enduring the same temptations. Yet neither they nor the world about them could forget the peculiar way in which they were a people for God's own possession.

Two groups are particularized for special mention along with the saints in Philippi, "bishops and deacons." The Greek word translated "bishop" means "overseer." Our "superintendent," derived from Latin, is almost an exact equivalent. Bishops were not a governing body but were men to whom the oversight of certain matters had been committed by the church. To the extent that a pastor or elder is charged with the supervision of a church, he is a bishop. Similarly, "deacons" are ministers of the church. The word is a transliteration of the Greek word for servants (John 2:5). The idea that deacons are to be a governing board in a church, ruling its policies and regulating its affairs, is foreign to the New Testament. It seeps in today from the methods practiced by business corporations which have their board of directors and an executive head. In the New Testament the honor and privilege attached to both groups is that of service (Mark 10:42-45).

Paul's greeting itself is: "Grace to you and peace from God our Father and the Lord Jesus Christ" (ASV). The ideas involved in these words are too great for treatment here, except to say that grace is the only adequate answer to the problem of sin (Rom. 5:20). For the present, we can simply call attention to the order that exists between the two great concepts of grace and peace. Grace always comes first, then peace. The world about us says much about peace but nothing about grace, and for that reason is a stranger to both. The Christian knows the order in which they come, and the source of both—the imperial Christ.

## II. "AND THIS I PRAY" (vv. 3-11)

The next paragraph before us begins and ends with praise: "I thank God . . . unto the glory and praise of God" (ASV). In the cycle between, the reader is drawn into Paul's awareness of God's good hand in all that befalls him. Praise and petition are commingled in perfect harmony.

### 1. *The Prayer of Praise* (vv. 3-7)

Praise is undoubtedly the highest expression of faith, and here it abounds with hope and love in a blend so perfect as to dispel the gloom of prison with the glory of heaven. Paul's paean of praise is well grounded. It rests upon remembrance (vv. 3-5) and assurance (vv. 5-7).

In the loneliness of every great affliction, memory serves a blessed purpose. Only God could know how often Paul had thought about his friends in Philippi during the long years of imprisonment and suffering. He pays them a noble tribute when he says that all his remembrance of them was an occasion of gratitude. The making of pleasant memories for ourselves and others should challenge our noblest endeavor. It may be that our friends cannot give thanks for every remembrance of us; but, by the grace of God, we can improve the record.

Paul made supplication for the Philippians with joy for their "fellowship in furtherance of the gospel from the first day until now" (v. 5 ASV). That kind of fellowship is the source of sweetest memories always. This "partnership" in the gospel was no idle thing. It began when

Lydia, the first convert, invited Paul and Silas and Timothy and Luke to make her place of business their headquarters for the preaching of the word in Macedonia. Through the more than ten years since, it had found many expressions, the last of which was the presence of Epaphroditus and the generous gift he had brought. There are many ways in which a person can further the gospel and by them all win the eternal gratitude, not only of those who are called to preach it, but also of those who are won by its saving power.

The assurance upon which Paul's prayer of praise rests is twofold: It stems from the nature of God, who can be counted on to finish what he begins (v. 6), and from the nature of their mutual experience of his grace, so genuine as to remove all hesitation whatsoever (v. 7).

Much of the timidity which keeps us playing about on the fringes of the Christian experience grows out of our failure to apprehend the nature of God, who initiates it. He can be counted on to finish what he has begun. "He who began a good work in you will perfect it [right on] until [its glorious consummation in] the day of Jesus Christ" (v. 6 ASV). To start a thing and then leave it is a weakness in any character and cannot be tolerated in the idea of God. He who inspires our faith will also perfect it (Heb. 12:2).

The only thing that can stay God's process of perfection is our unbelief. And even when our smoking lamps are flickering in the darkness, he does not quench them, for, as the prophet Isaiah says, "He will not fail nor be discouraged, till he have set justice in the earth; and the isles shall wait for his law" (Isa. 42:4 ASV). Paul's heart is buoyant because he knows the Architect and, beyond the scaffolding and the litter necessary to the process of construction, can see the building taking shape according to plan.

Paul feels a perfect right to be thus assured as he looks out upon the level of human circumstances. The bond between him and the Philippians is genuine. Each is in the other's heart, for the wording of verse 7 in the Greek is purposely ambiguous so as to mean either, "I have you in my heart" or "Ye have me in your heart." In any case the bond between them will hold through fair weather and foul, for it is of God's own making. They are partners with him both in his chains and in the affirmation and the confirmation of the gospel of grace. Their comradeship adds to the fervor of his praise.

## 2. *The Prayer of Petition* (vv. 8-11)

Paul introduces his prayer of petition by describing the longing out of which it grows. His words are sober and earnest as he calls God to witness his longing for them in the "tender mercies of Christ" (v. 8 ASV). This is a happier translation than the more literal expression found in the King James Version, which reads, "I long after you all in the bowels of Jesus Christ." "The ancient Greeks located the emotions of love, pity, joy, etc., in the 'stomach-brain,' as it is sometimes called." [1] The point to notice is the intensity of Paul's love and longing for the Philippians. This verse should be sufficient answer for those who decry emotion in religion. Paul feels the very yearning of Christ's own compassion stirring his soul in their behalf, and has employed the strongest figures at his command to express it. The vigor of our prayer life will be found always in the intensity of our desires.

The next three verses give the prayer itself (v. 9) and the purpose in asking it (vv. 10-11). Since prayers in general are revealing, and Paul's especially so, we shall

---

[1] A. T. Robertson, *Paul's Joy in Christ*, p. 66.

linger awhile over this petition, indulging in a bit of word study to catch its deeper meaning.

"And this I am praying—that your love [which has found such beautiful expression all along] may abound yet more and more in complete understanding and all discernment" (v. 9).[2] Love is the thing for emphasis. The love of God poured forth in Paul's heart through the Holy Spirit which was given him (Rom. 5:5) could be satisfied with nothing less than that love returned from the hearts of others. Through the years past, it had found varied and beautiful expression from the saints in Philippi. Paul recognized this, but he desired that it overflow increasingly, more and more. It was to be channeled in "knowledge and all discernment," that they might distinguish between the things that differ.

Nothing heightens the faculties of discernment like love. There is a saying from the days of Shakespeare that love is blind. But that is not the case. It is those who do not love who are blind. A girl in love is not blind to the faults in her fiance which may be so obvious to others; but because her eyes are opened by love, she is able to perceive his worth, and the things to which others have taken exception become inconsequential by comparison. Love sharpens all our capacities of perception. It is not hard to understand people whom we love. We can catch their meaning in a glance or a smile or hear it in the overtones of their speech. Paul knew this held true in the things of God, and he wanted the Philippians prepared to lay hold on the higher values he had in store for them.

---

[2] Wherever a Scripture passage is not indicated as being from the American Standard Version (ASV), the translation is the work of the author.

The Greek words for "knowledge" and "discernment" repay careful study. Since we are accustomed to "diagnosis" for knowledge of a very thorough sort, and to "prognosis" for a knowledge so accurate as to predict the course of a disease, why not make room in our vocabulary for *epignosis*, which is a transliteration of the very word used here? It suggests knowledge heaped up as in a pile, one fact upon another, and the possessor on top of it all. A man in such a position is supported by all the facts in the case, and that is what Paul is after.

The other word, translated "discernment," is that from which "esthetic" is derived. The overtones of a rich emotional life are present in this "science of the beautiful." One develops a feeling for the finer distinctions that constitute real art. This faculty is more a matter of the heart than of the head. And by it one can come to know the intuitive leadings of the Spirit and sense what is, and what is not, pleasing to him long before the issue involved is plain enough to be reasoned through. Love sensitizes the soul and makes man receptive to all the finer distinctions in God's revealed truth.

The immediate effect sought in this prayer is explained in the first part of verse 10, "so that ye may approve the things that are excellent" (ASV). Approval is the next step after knowledge and all discernment. Actually there are three stages to the idea in the word translated "approve." The meaning in the first stage is "to test," and it is illustrated by the use of this same word in 1 John 4:1, "Beloved, believe not every spirit, but *prove* the spirits, whether they are of God" (ASV). (See also 1 Thess. 5:21.) The idea involved in the second stage is that found in the text we are studying, "approve." For the meaning to be found in the third stage, we will turn to the famous exhortation to consecration in Romans 12:1-2, which concludes: " . . . that ye may *prove* what is the good and acceptable and perfect will of God" (ASV). The idea in this final stage differs from that in the first in that the will of God must be proved by experience as good and acceptable and perfect.

Many years ago when there was little currency in use in China and almost all purchases were made in cash, the merchants would keep a smooth block of polished marble or stone on their counters conveniently near the cash drawer. There were so many counterfeits among the silver coins which were passed that the merchant, if he had the slightest suspicion, would fling the coin upon the smooth stone. If it did not have the right "ring," he would not hesitate to return it and ask for another. If its tone marked it as genuine silver, he would put it in the drawer, and the transaction would be completed.

So much that is counterfeit is being passed over life's counters that God wants his children skilled in the art of discernment. They must first test, then approve, and finally ring up in the cash drawer of experience the coinage of truth, which is the medium of exchange for real riches. In a world where values differ so widely, the Christian whose ability to discriminate has not been sensitized by the love of God and by the love of his truth is utterly at a loss.

It takes real discernment to distinguish between the "things that differ" as the phrase before us, "the things that are excellent," might well be translated. In the reading of this very letter Paul wanted the Philippians to appreciate the distinction that exists between the many interpretations of life's harsh circumstances. Only thus can one ever recognize the opportunity that comes with every affliction.

God has ordered all our trials to enrich our lives if only we can recognize the gifts these trials bear. Paul

wished to pass on to others the difference he had found
between rejoicing in the Lord and rejoicing in the favor-
able circumstances that sometimes attend the ways of
those who trust God. He wanted the readers of his
letter to learn also the difference between being in Christ
and out of Christ, between fruit and works, between
peace with God and the peace of God. Such discernment is the key to wealth.

The over-all purpose of this prayer is summed up in
verse 11, the last verse of the paragraph we shall study
in this chapter. It leads us from discernment to achievement—out of the realm of value into the realm of character, the highest realm of all. Here the emphasis is upon
what men are, not upon what they have or know. There
is a day coming, "the day of Christ," in which men will
be revealed for what they are. This is Paul's second
reference in these eleven verses to that day, and serves to
show the influence it had upon all his estimates and en-
deavors.

He prayed that in the clear light of that day the Philippians might be found "sincere and void of offence."
Our English word "sincere" is from the Latin word
which means "without wax." It refers to a trick of sculp-
tors, to hide with wax the defects wrought by an errant
chisel. To be sincere means to be without camouflage
or tricks of the trade designed to deceive the eye, of
man. Paul is mindful of the difference between character
and reputation, and wants no blemish of character or
occasion of stumbling to appear in them in the light of
judgment.

The paragraph ends on the positive note of praise.
Like the saints in Philippi we are to be "filled with the
fruit of righteousness that is through Jesus Christ, unto
the glory and praise of God" (v. 11). Observe that the
word translated "fruits" is in the singular number as the

margin of the American Revi
reminds us instantly of Gala
fruit of the Spirit is contraste
flesh. The force of the figure
of grace achievement is to be ;
works. The work of grace v
human heart through Jesus Cl
the fruitage of praise and gl
demption becomes complete.

## QUESTIONS FOR REVIEW AND EXAMINATION

1. What can you discover about Paul's personality from
   the salutation to this letter?

2. In Philippians 1:3-7 try to find and list all the reasons Paul gave for offering praise, even when he was
   in prison. Check those which you can honestly claim
   as reasons for praise in your own life.

3. As you study Philippians 1:8-11, with the help of the
   discussion in this chapter, try to write out each of
   Paul's petitions, expressing it in words which are
   common today.

# Chapter V

# FOLLOWING THE FORTUNES
# OF THE GOSPEL

One need not be a skilful navigator to chart the course which Paul takes in the verses from Philippians under treatment in this chapter. The beacons are numerous and their signals so strong that it would be hard to wander off the beam. The more conspicuous markers are "the progress of the gospel," "manifest in Christ," "speak the word," "preach Christ," "defence of the gospel," "proclaim Christ," "Christ is proclaimed," "Christ . . . magnified," "your progress and joy in the faith," "worthy of the gospel of Christ." Such phrases as these line out the course unmistakably. Paul is discussing the fortunes of the gospel, with which he has become completely identified, but actually he seems not so much concerned with his direction as with the thrill of the ride.

To change the figure, he is riding the ground swell of God's victory in the gospel, and though the watery elements beneath him may curl and buckle and crash into a million flecks of foam, that impulse sweeping in from the fathomless sea of God's love will bear him in triumph to the golden strand. His joy in this section of the letter is the elation of one to whom all things work together for good because his destiny is inseparably linked with that of the gospel.

## I. Things That Happen (vv. 12-18.)

"The things which happened unto me" (v. 12 ASV) represents the best our translators could do with a neat idiom of eight letters in the Greek. Actually the verb "happened" is not in the original, but the idea is there. Paul naturally wants his readers informed as to the events that have transpired and their effect upon the progress of the Word.

Things that happen! Much is included in that phrase. It describes a vast area bounded by theologians in terms of God's permissive will. Look at the things that had happened to Paul: thwarted in the purpose of his offering from the Gentile churches; mobbed in Jerusalem; plotted against and unjustly imprisoned, a pawn in the chess game between two Roman governors and the Jews; shipwrecked, all but destitute; chained to a guard in his own hired dwelling. Now, after four long years, he hopes against hope for release. These are the things that had happened to him because he linked his destiny with that of the gospel, and if their meaning is to be understood, they must be viewed in the light of the purpose for which God permitted them, that he might use them for the furtherance of the saving Word.

### 1. *As to the World Without* (v. 13)

Paul says that it has now become plain, not only to "the whole praetorian guard" but also to all the rest, that his bonds are worn for Christ's sake and not for some crime of his own commitment, as in the case of the other prisoners. This is progress indeed, for the significance of one's sacrifice is determined by the altar upon which it is placed (Matt. 23:19), and thus even the heathen soldiers who guarded him could not be impervious to the meaning of Paul's hardships.

According to some authorities, in the days of the emperor Tiberius there were ten thousand soldiers, the very flower of the Roman army, stationed in Rome. Whether Paul's reference here is to a company like them is not quite certain. One thing, however, is crystal-clear: Paul used his contacts with these soldiers and others to win them to Jesus. As one guard would relieve another, Paul's daily witness came to be felt throughout the whole company and in other quarters in Rome. Later, in response to the call of duty, these very men would be stationed in distant areas of the far-flung empire and would bear the word of salvation to others. Though not of his choosing, the conditions under which he lived in Rome supplied the missionary-prisoner with the very finest contacts, and he gloried in them all.

## 2. As to the Brotherhood of Believers (vv. 14-17)

The heroic interpretation which Paul gave to his surroundings had its effect also upon the believers who were in Rome. Encouraged by his example, the great majority of them spoke out more boldly. If fear is contagious, so is courage. Paul was an inspiration to all who visited him or heard about him, and his presence in Rome, even in bonds, put iron into the blood of some who were growing fainthearted under the threat of persecution. This is the joy of making a resolute stand for Christ. A man's influence under such circumstances extends far beyond anything of which he is aware at the time.

But there were some who, instead of being encouraged by Paul's example, were incited by it. These were critics of his, perhaps Jewish Christians still clinging to the idea that one must enter the Christian fold by way of Mosaic ceremonialism. They knew that Paul's heart was set like a flint for the defense of the gospel of grace, and they thought to raise additional trouble for him by the version of Christ which they preached. Dr. A. T. Robertson suggests they may have been leaders in the work before Paul's arrival who became jealous of the prominence which became his.[1] At any rate the motives which prompted them were not sincere, and their activity was but sham behind which they hid their envy and strife from others and perhaps from themselves. These verses search our own motives; they also hold up Paul's courage as an inspiration for all who endure the hardships which are bound to follow an all-out stand for Christ.

### 3. *As to Paul Himself* (v. 18)

Paul sums up the construction he will place on this perplexing problem of mixed motives by expressing his joy that "whether in pretence or in truth" Christ is being proclaimed. After all, that is the thing that counts. "Somehow God blesses the grain of truth that is mixed in with error and bad motives. . . . He [Paul] does not rejoice in false preaching, but in the fact that even in such preaching Christ is found by souls that hunger after Him."[2]

Through Paul's experience we can see the approach God would have us make to things that happen in the realm of his permissive will. Their values are to be determined always by God's prevailing purpose, "the progress of the gospel" (v. 12 ASV). A mother whose heart was crushed by a tragedy which happened through no fault of her own, wrote her pastor, "Your advice to stop asking *why* helped a lot. And your sermon yesterday helped to make us able to say, 'I will,' and leave it in God's hands.

---

[1] *Paul's Joy in Christ*, p. 82.

[2] *Ibid*, p. 89.

We will just let Him use *even this,* till his plan is per-
fected." And then she added this bit of verse, her own
triumphant expression of a faith purified in the fires of
adversity:

> The things that happen unto me
> Are not by chance I know—
> But because my Father's wisdom
> Has willed to have it so.
> For the "furtherance of the gospel"
> As a part of His great plan,
> God can use our disappointments
> And the weaknesses of man.
>
> Give me faith to meet them bravely
> Trials I do not understand,
> To let God work His will in me—
> To trust His guiding hand.
> Help me to shine, a clear bright light,
> And not to live in vain—
> Help me hold forth the Word of life
> In triumph over pain.

MRS. J. S. KING

## II. SALVATION, THE END RESULT (vv. 19-20)

The point of view shifts from the present to the future
toward the close of verse 18. Here Paul raises his Eben-
ezer, exclaiming in joy, "Hitherto hath Jehovah helped us"
(1 Sam. 7:12 ASV). But this marker along the pilgrimage always points forward; and because experience of
God's grace supplies assurance, Paul looks to the future
with confident joy: "For I know that [all] this shall turn
out to my salvation" (v. 19 ASV). The translators rightly
make this an affirmation of faith by the use of a future
tense form indicating strong determination. "Salvation"
here is to be understood in its larger sense as including
Paul's welfare not only hereafter but also in this present

life. God delivers us from the predicaments into which he permits us to fall.

Two prepositions in the Greek, translated "through" and "according to," indicate respectively the means of this deliverance and the measure to which it may be enjoyed. Taken with the phrases they introduce, they will repay careful study, because there is no problem which presses more immediately upon us than that occasioned by life's predicaments.

### 1. *The Means* (v. 19)

The channels through which deliverance comes are prayer and the supply of the Spirit of Jesus Christ. The blood-bought privilege of prayer is the door God has opened through which we may leave the realm of his permissive will, where almost anything can happen, and enter the realm of his active will, where everything that takes place falls into line with his sovereign purpose.[3] Paul was a man of prayer and relied strongly on the prayers of others.

Closely linked with this ministry of intercession—actually inspiring it—was the supply of the Spirit of Jesus Christ. God never allows his children to be cut off from their source of supply. The presence of his Spirit in their hearts is the never-failing guarantee of all needed strength and wisdom for any emergency. The history of the word translated "supply" dates back to the days in ancient Greece when some wealthy patron of the arts footed the bill for the chorus, or cast, in a drama. Sometimes directly, sometimes through the prayers and ministry of others, always unfailingly, God's Spirit supplies the needs of everyone who takes his part in the unfolding drama of redemption.

---

[3] Oswald Chambers, *If Ye Shall Ask*.

## 2. *The Measure* (v. 20)

Paul's own response in all of this was another factor to be considered in the outcome. The preposition translated "according to" indicates that the degree of success depended largely upon his own attitude, which he describes as one of "earnest expectation and hope." Of the Greek word used here Dr. A. T. Robertson says: "A very strong and striking word . . . used for intent watching with head bent or stretched in that direction. It occurs in the papyri of the expectation of peasants about the visit . . . of a high official." [4] The picture comes to mind of the trademark of a certain recording company— a dog with head cocked to one side in puzzled alertness, listening to "his master's voice." Sometimes it takes intentness of that nature to detect the plan which the Master hand is weaving into the pattern of our circumstances. The glory of the outcome will justify all it costs, and to the fulfilment of his part in it Paul looked with steadfast hope.

His part was to magnify Christ—living and dying were incidental to that grand purpose. The world has learned a great deal about magnification since Paul first used this expressive figure. Today a two-hundred-inch telescope searches the skies from the summit of Mount Palomar, California, more than six thousand feet above sea level. This giant eye brings the far-flung inhabitants of space nearer by billions of miles. One who has seen the moons of Jupiter or the flaming band of Saturn can never forget the feeling of awe that overtook him as, for the first time, their glory dawned upon him through the lenses of a telescope. The telescope, however, adds nothing to that which was there already; it only makes

---

[4] *Op. cit.*, p. 90, footnote.

its grandeur visible to the eye of man. So it is with our lives when we magnify the glories of Christ.

᷾We magnify Christ by making him visible to those who could not see him otherwise. A Christian physician, successful in her career and highly respected by her profession, was relating to a group of friends how she had come to meet Jesus, whose power to save had transformed her life. One of the steps that led her out from the atheism she once boasted was the manner in which a young Christian husband and his wife received a great disappointment. "It was a hard thing to tell them," she said. "I knew how they had longed for children to gladden their hearts and home, and now their hopes were blasted. But it was the way they took it that impressed me. I knew that God was real to them. I was haunted by the realization that they had something I did not possess—and I wanted it."

Friends of the young couple doubtless offered their sympathy and superficially charged the whole experience off as "one of those things that happen." Perhaps even the husband and wife themselves do not know that in the hour of their anguish God focused the lenses of their heartache in such a way that the glory of Christ's redeeming love flashed in upon the eye of an unbeliever. But in heaven's bright light they will see how it turned out to them for salvation—their own in a larger sense, and that of a physician whose witness in her church and community is increasingly a power for Christ.

## III. WEIGHING LIFE'S ALTERNATIVES (vv. 21-26)

In an earlier chapter we discussed quite at length the meaning of Paul's classic phrase, "For to me to live is Christ, and to die is gain" (v. 21 ASV). The thing to note here is that this conception of the Christian life is not balanced (except by implication) against a life without Christ. The two alternatives which constitute Paul's dilemma are whether to live on here (in the flesh) or to depart and be with Christ, which, of course, would mean physical death. No man is at his best till he calmly faces either eventuality. To do so is to discover that the Christian occupies a heads-I-win-tails-you-lose position in reference to anything Satan can do. In either case, Paul stood to win.

### 1. *"Betwixt the Two"* (vv. 22-23)

To depart and be with Christ Paul sets down immediately as "gain." It yields the twin advantages of release from the weariness of continual strife here and realization of the fulness of joy in the presence of Christ. Paul's conception of what takes place for the Christian after the death of his body admits of no "soul sleep" or intermediary period of probation. To him, when the earthly tent folds up, its occupant moves immediately into a "house not made with hands, eternal, in the heavens" (2 Cor. 5:1 ASV).

Thus, "to be absent from the body" is to be "at home with the Lord" (2 Cor. 5:8). It is Paul the traveler, however, who speaks in Philippians, rather than Paul the tentmaker. The word for "depart" in verse 23 has a nautical usage and means "to weigh anchor." Many a saint has shared Paul's longing quietly to slip the moorings of this life and set sail for the haven beyond the portals of death. One thinks of Tennyson's classic poem "Crossing the Bar," and the sublime music of Richard Strauss's *Death and Transfiguration.*

Life hereafter is a beautiful thing for the Christian. Foretastes of its joys are experienced even here. Paul had already been caught up in holy ecstasy into paradise, where he heard "words that cannot, and indeed must not, be translated into human speech" (2 Cor. 12:4 Phillips).

In the passage before us he describes the status of those who depart to be with Christ as "very far better" in comparison to anything experienced here. In this respect his words are like those of Jesus, who said, "If it were not so, I would have told you" (John 14:2 ASV). Both of them slip the halter from our imaginations to let them roam in free anticipation of the bliss that awaits us in the Father's house of many mansions.

## 2. *The Choice of Faith* (vv. 24-26)

But Paul was no escapist indulging in idle dreams about heaven. His thoughts of the afterlife were geared in a very practical way into the needs of the present. The time would come when in the quiet countryside along the Ostian Road the headsman's ax would release his spirit to be "at home with the Lord," but only after he had finished his course here (2 Tim. 4:6-8). Now there was work to be done. To live on in the flesh meant continued fruit from his labor and was more needful for the sake of those to whom he was writing. With this in mind his confidence in God's power to deliver tipped the beam in favor of staying on with them. "I know that I shall abide, yea, and abide with you all [be released from prison and join you again], for your progress and joy in the faith" (v. 25 ASV). His reunion with them would fill their cup of joy to overflowing and would be also one more trophy of God's power in Christ over which they could exult together (v. 26).

## IV. THE GOSPEL-WORTHY LIFE (vv. 27-30)

Paul's appeal in the remaining verses of this chapter is to a life that matches the glorious destiny of the gospel which he has just outlined. The quality of their daily living is his one great concern. In the previous verses the figure of scales came to mind as one possibility was balanced against another. That picture occurs again in the word translated "worthy." "Only worthily of the gospel of Christ behave as citizens" (v. 27). The adverb is derived from a stem meaning "to lead," and the story of how it came to mean "worthily" is most interesting and instructive. On a pair of scales, of course, an accepted standard of measurement was used to determine the weight of the substance against which it was matched. The "worth" was found as the standard weight drew or led the beam to a horizontal balance. The privileges available to us in the gospel must be matched by our behavior as Christian citizens.

This gospel-worthy life is described in verses 27-28 as independent, vigorous, and courageous. Regardless of whether or not he was restored to them, Paul wanted them to press right on in the direction he had outlined. He wanted them to be able to stand alone without the prop of his presence. The ability of this great missionary to wean his converts and set them on their own is one of the astonishing things about him. It marks him in sharp contrast to many today who prolong the babyhood of those to whom they minister in order to satisfy their own vanity by seeming necessary. They are flattered instead of rebuked by twenty-year-old babes in Christ who say, "We just couldn't get along without you." There was not a member of the Philippian church who had been a Christian more than ten years, and yet that church set a high-mark of achievement in the things of Christ, to which we, with all our centuries of Christian heritage, can but aspire.

Paul accepted life's disciplines himself, and for that reason he did not hesitate to require discipline in others. Regardless of circumstances the Philippian Christians must learn to "stand together" in one spirit and to "strive together with one mind for the faith of the gospel." Our word "athlete" is derived from a part of the word translated "striving." Their efforts together must show the teamwork of trained athletes. Nor can they allow themselves to be startled, or stampeded, by the first sign of opposition from their adversaries. The Christian element is of sterner stuff than that and resolutely calls the bluff of Satan's show of strength. The concluding verse in this passage indicates that the conflict is the same—as the privilege of having a part in it is also the same—whether in Rome or in Philippi, whether then or now.

The Greek text of Westcott and Hort places a parenthesis around the following words: "which is for them an evident token of perdition, but of your salvation, and that from God; because to you it hath been granted [as the bestowing of a privilege] in the behalf of Christ, not only to believe on him, but also to suffer in his behalf" (ASV). The thought is parenthetical. It gives the twofold meaning of persecution, which is at once a sign of perdition and of privilege: "Perdition for them," Paul says, "but privilege for you." The privilege of suffering may fall as a strange note upon the human ear, but the veteran apostle sounds it clearly. Attention is directed to it now because it will appear again in the next movement in this symphonic poem of love, joy and peace, which we call Philippians.

## Questions for Review and Examination

1. Tell two ways in which Paul's imprisonment had caused the progress of the gospel (Phil. 1: 12-18).

2. Why could Paul be assured that good would come to him out of his imprisonment? Through what two channels would deliverance come (v. 19)? What did Paul's own attitude have to do with the good which

he would get out of his experience (v. 20)? Do you think our attitude determines, in part, how much blessing we get out of suffering or difficulty?

3. As you read verse 29, ask yourself if you consider suffering a privilege. Review verses 12-18 to find truths to help you rejoice even in the midst of tribulation. List these truths.

# CHAPTER VI

# CHRIST-MINDEDNESS

## PHILIPPIANS 2

The second chapter of Philippians falls naturally into three divisions as indicated by the three paragraphs of the American Standard Version (vv. 1-11, 12-18, 19-30). The underlying theme, however, which gives them unity and justifies their treatment here in one chapter is a bit difficult to trace. We will do well to assign the third paragraph (vv. 19-30) to matters purely personal—plans more or less incidental so far as doctrines are concerned. And yet, these plans for Timothy and Epaphroditus radiate the same joyous spirit which characterizes the doctrinal portions of the letter, and fall quite naturally in a section, introduced by Paul's reference to his circumstances in Philippians 1:12.

The kinship between the first and second paragraphs is closer, both of them developing and applying the theme introduced in the preceding chapter. The sense in which Paul uses the word "salvation" in 2:12 echoes that of 1:19, as he challenges them to work out their own salvation, even as he was in the process of working out his. The sublime heights reached in verses 1-11 are but an amplification of the truth presented in 1:28-29, that beyond the privilege of believing on Jesus lies the even greater privilege of suffering in his behalf.

Thus far we have seen how the apostle Paul exults in a life identified with the assured successes of the gospel. Linked with its fortunes, he rides his circumstances in victory. But the viewpoint hitherto has been from the manward side, and there is another point of view. How does the gospel look to one who has not fallen a victim to sin? Has it anything to offer one who has escaped man's predicament or whose position was from the beginning superior to it? Paul makes this daring shift in viewpoint as he discloses the *Christ-mindedness* of verses 5-8. There one looks at the death-life principle of the gospel from the Godward side. The joy it affords is one into which Christ himself entered. It is a sobering thought that before ever the gospel presented its opportunity to man, it unfolded an opportunity which God himself welcomed. The joy latent in its eternal message was considered first in the counsels of the Godhead, and embraced before the foundation of the world by Father, Son, and Holy Spirit.

There is, therefore, nothing arbitrary about the conditions which the gospel imposes upon wayward man. The condemnation of sin and the necessity of repentance are both expressions of the love which the gospel reveals. Love works on the death-life principle; it grows by its self-giving. Its choice of the cross is natural. Man should obey the gospel, therefore, not because it is the only means of escape from the penalty of sin, though that is true. He should obey the gospel for the same reason that Christ was obedient to it, because this is the way of abounding joy. And when man's obedience partakes of this Christ-mindedness, the fountain of his joy will spring, not from the circumstances of his deliverance, but from the heart of God. Christ-mindedness, then, is that attitude which sees in the cross, not the necessity only, but the privilege also—the sure way of self-realization for the sinner as it was for the Son of God.

If the reader feels that such a point of view as we have been discussing is too far removed from the realities of this practical world, he needs but to examine the phrases in which this sublime revelation is couched. There is nothing more practical than to look beyond necessity to privilege. To do so supplies the very breath of inspiration; it dignifies the menial and transfigures the commonplace with the glory of heaven. Not for a moment does the grandeur of Paul's outlook cause his feet to stumble as he walks the lowly path of service.

## I. THE APPEAL SUPREME (vv. 1-11)

"Deep calleth unto deep at the noise of thy waterfalls" (Psalm 42:7 ASV). Like appeals to like, and on this principle so beautifully stated by the psalmist, Paul proceeds to dig beneath the surface for that which is fundamental in the Christian experience. If we may borrow a figure from travel in more recent times, he is about to give their mired-down car a mighty tug, and he wants to be sure he ties on to something that won't pull loose.

### 1. *Its Basis* (v. 1)

Paul appeals to that which is basic. The fourfold occurrence of the phrase "if any" reveals those characteristics which in the eyes of Paul mark a Christian experience as genuine. He does not ask for shibboleths of doctrinal statements or reasoned explanations. Rather, he asks for evidences which stem directly from within, experiences which show the immediacy of their fellowship with Christ and flood the whole of their being with the warmth of his love. He digs under the surface of outward professions for their "encouragement" in Christ, the "tender persuasiveness" of their love, for their "partnership" with the Spirit, and for all that is sweet and tender in their emotions. Thus he escapes the tragedy of superficial appeals which are the blight of so much exhortation today. "Deep calleth unto deep." God always appeals to the best there is in us.

## 2. *Its Joyful Nature* (vv. 2-4)

Paul pleads for an overflowing cup of joy because the thirst of his holy ambition for them can never be quite satisfied. He is like John, who wrote to Gaius, "Greater joy have I none than this, to hear of my children walking in the truth" (3 John 4 ASV). In a series of sharp contrasts three verses describe precisely what it would take on their part to fill Paul's cup of joy to overflowing: unity, humility, and charity.

The unity which Paul sought for them was to come about as they looked at life from the same point of view. They were to have the same "mind," or attitude. Four times (once in a compound, "lowliness of mind") does this word "mind" occur in these verses under study. The idea is not so much that of one's intellectual grasp as of one's disposition or attitude. The differences which so often mar our fellowship are attributable more to an unwillingness to see the problem from another's viewpoint than from difficulties in the problem itself. Pride enters in to complicate matters because a man "loses face" when he surrenders his position before others. Hence the need for humility. True understanding is like water in that it seeks the lowest level. A proud man has few teachers. It takes a humble heart to know the mind of God, but that is what Paul covets for the Philippians.

Love must have its part also in the accord which Paul seeks. Its presence is indicated in verse 2 and its work described in the first part of verse 3 and again in verse 4. Party pride, empty boasting, and seeking one's own interests to the exclusion of others, are all too common symptoms of the dread disease of selfishness. On the defensive, self strikes back in jealous strife or scurries to cover under pompous boasts; on the offensive, it surveys the field only in terms of its own advantage. Love is God's specific antidote for this malady. "Love envieth not; love vaunteth not itself, . . . seeketh not its own" (1 Cor. 13:4-5 ASV). By the little word "also" (Phil. 2: 4) Paul indicates that a man may rightly look to his own interests, but not at the expense of others.

We gather from such an appeal that however nobly the Philippians manifested the Christian graces, they were still far from perfect. They were beset by the same infirmities that assail us. The church then was not a place for perfect people, nor is it now. But the letters of the New Testament are written in such a way that the imperfections of those early Christians become the means which God uses to present the ideal for them and for us. And that ideal challenges, rather than mocks, our endeavor, because with its revelation God supplies the grace for achievement.

### 3. *Christ, Its Sublime Inspiration* (vv. 5-11)

We shall do well to loose the sandals from our feet as we approach the next six verses, for we stand on holy ground. The late Dr. W. Hersey Davis has described Philippians 2:5-11 as "the sublimest passage in Paul about the person of Christ." Its grandeur is more readily visible to the heart than to the head. It is not too difficult to analyze the steps leading to this lofty height, but one may miss the sublimity of the total picture if he looks too closely at them. The Matterhorn comes repeatedly to mind, rising, snow-clad, in solitary grandeur above the peaks surrounding it.

(1) *His preincarnate state* (v. 6).—Verse 6 is a contemplation of Christ before he came "out of the ivory palaces into a world of woe." The vistas of eternity unfold in the word translated "existing," which denotes Christ's existence prior to his entrance into time. John says, "In the beginning was the Word, and the Word was with God, and the Word was God" (John 1:1 ASV).

From eternity the Son was coexistent with the Father, enjoying an equality with him both in the dignity of that position and in the very "form," or essential nature of deity itself. One is not surprised that some of the expressions in this passage have occasioned controversy among the theologians who have, under the guidance of God's Spirit, wrought out the Christology in general acceptance today. Our attention must not be sidetracked by controversy but kept in focus upon the chief point for emphasis, namely: What was Christ's attitude toward his position in reference to the death-life principle that was to become revealed in the gospel of grace?

(2) *His* kenosis, *or self-emptying* (vv. 6-8).—That attitude is described in the phrase, "[he] counted [it] not . . . a thing to be grasped" (v. 6 ASV). The quaint translation of the King James Version, "thought it not robbery," is quite expressive if one takes the time to see the picture it presents. The preincarnate Christ did not regard the advantage of his position as something to be held on to at all costs, greedily grasped as a robber seizes his plunder. Rather, he regarded it as something to be readily relinquished for the higher gain and the greater glory which would become his through obedience to the death-life principle of the cross.

It was this attitude which Paul underscored for the Philippians and for us. This is the "mind of Christ" which we are to have. The self-emptying process unfolded in verses 7 and 8 stems from this point of view. We must leave to the theologians the distinction between manifest deity and essential deity involved in the Greek word "to make empty." The poet Charles Wesley has expressed its truth for us in two phrases which every heart understands: "Mild He lays His glory by," and "Veiled in flesh the God-head see." The thing to watch is Christ's descent from glory as, round by round, he makes his way downward into the depths. He who had existed in the form of God now takes the form of a slave, "being made [becoming] in the likeness of men." And "being found in fashion [all outward appearance] as a man," he further humbled himself, "becoming obedient [as one who hears from a subordinate position] . . . unto death [and that, not just any death but], . . . the *death of the cross*" (ASV). From the throne of glory to the cross of shame!

> Oh, the love that drew salvation's plan!
> Oh, the grace that brought it down to man!
> Oh, the mighty gulf that God did span
> At Calvary!

W. R. NEWELL

(3) *His exaltation* (vv. 9-11).—"Wherefore also God highly exalted him" (v. 9). Never has a "wherefore" been more deeply rooted or more satisfying to reason. There is a law of the spiritual universe frequently stated in the Bible: "Everyone that exalteth himself shall be humbled; and he that humbleth himself shall be exalted" (Luke 14:11 ASV). Jesus gave voice to that law in the home of a Pharisee and fulfilled it on Calvary and in his glorious ascension from the Mount of Olives. The exaltation here described carries us beyond the glory-cloud which received him out of the disciples' sight, and beyond this age to one when he shall reign in manifest victory.

The two elements in this exaltation are the bestowing of a name, earned now that the man Christ Jesus has merged the life-stream of the human race with that of God (v. 9), and the recognition of that name on the part of every created intelligence whether in heaven or on earth or under the earth (vv. 10-11). It is satisfying to know that before him every knee shall bow and that every tongue shall confess to the glory of God the Father that Jesus Christ is Lord.

We cannot leave this classic passage without calling attention to the simplicity, the transparency, the charm of perfect naturalness, that marks our Lord's descent from glory. The Water of life flows without sediment of self, crystal-clear. Our Saviour's humility finds such ready acceptance because it was so natural. It was not an assumed or an affected selflessness, as it is so often with us—a condescension which offends those whom it would serve. Rather, it was an expression of self, the true self, rejoicing in the privilege of finding and giving the highest good. However humble his service, whether talking with the sinful woman at Jacob's well or bathing the dusty feet of his disciples or bearing his cross, what Jesus did was never stilted. That is what amazes and charms us. Why should he be stilted? One is most at ease when he is most himself. From this point of view he was acting in terms of his own holy self-realization. It was for the joy that was set before him that he endured the cross, despising its shame (Heb. 12:2).

Our conception of self is one thing that keeps us from understanding Philippians 2:1-11. To us, self is bad, almost synonymous with sin; but not to God, nor yet to that which he has redeemed. We speak of the "true self," the "higher self," and so forth, but our vision is impaired by the havoc sin has wrought. It is hard for us to conceive of anyone, even of Christ, acting in self-interest without being "selfish." We subordinate our wills to God's with such little grace and with so much ado because we lack the mind of Christ, which sees that God's will is the fulfilment of our life and that the privilege in it far outweighs the pain.

## II. "Your Own Salvation" (vv. 12-18)

"So then . . . " The sublime example of Christ is cited for very practical reasons. Like Browning's musician in "Abt Vogler," Paul, after surveying the heights, finds "the common chord," his resting place, "the C Major of this life." What follows is linked with that which precedes by the word "obey." Christ's obedience to the death-life principle of the cross is the inspiration for our obedience.

### 1. *A Part for Each* (vv. 12-13)

The emphasis in verse 12 falls naturally upon "*your own* salvation." Paul appeals to their own sense of responsibility in this vast process of redemption, because spiritual maturity and accountability must go hand in hand. Evasion of responsibility is typical of that prolonged adolescence which would have blighted the work at Philippi as it has done in so many churches today. In the verses before us Paul advances three factors to stimulate the Philippians to work out their own salvation. The very logic of the situation is his first appeal. This is brought out by the word translated "so then."

The second factor is that there, in prisoner's bonds, Paul is successfully working out his own part in God's process of redemption, and from the heights of glory the Son of God has triumphantly wrought his unique part in this same process. The Christians in Philippi, therefore, simply could not fail to come up with the part God had left to them. Thus Paul's enforced absence from them becomes a challenge to encourage their response: "now much more in my absence."

The third factor is the divine initiative. This is the most powerful appeal of all: "God it is who is working in you both to will and to do according to his good pleasure" (v. 13).

Paul's conception of the divine initiative is always in terms that stimulate our own. In Romans 9-11, where this doctrine finds its fullest expression, God's sovereignty heightens man's free choice instead of paralyzing it. Engraved on the keystone of the arch constructed in those three chapters on the divine initiative are the words, "Whosoever shall call upon the name of the Lord shall be saved" (Rom. 10:13 ASV). Paul's conception of the doctrine of election spurs him to the most intense missionary activity. The same principle applies in the passage before us. The fact that it is God who works in us cannot lead to passivity on our part. Our choices and our actions are never freer and never more active than when thus engaged in the doing of his good pleasure. "But Paul gives the divine sovereignty as the reason or ground for the human free agency. He exhorts the Philippians to work out their own salvation with fear and trembling precisely because God works in them both the willing and the doing and for His good pleasure." [1]

## 2. *The Process Unfolded* (vv. 14-18)

This outworking of God's inworking is now described in terms of their own experience and of its effect upon others. For the Philippians it was to be a perfectly natural unfolding of the life which was in them, or, to follow Paul's shift of figures, it was to be the clear shining of the light which was theirs by virtue of their relation to Christ. In either figure the emphasis was on the transparency of their life. They were to do all things without murmuring and arguing ("questionings") because such expressions would obscure any thought of privilege in the inconveniences and hardships they were called upon to endure for Christ's sake.

---

[1] Robertson, *Paul's Joy in Christ*, p. 146.

No one murmurs at a privilege. Complaining Christians have never caught the vision of the cross. The generation in the midst of which the Christian lives is crooked (v. 15), all twisted up by the havoc of sin which has plunged the world into darkness. In this spiritual blackout the Christian's testimony shines forth with the Word of life.

In the latter portion of verse 16 and continuing on through the remaining verses of the paragraph, Paul weighs the effect of such a witness upon himself and the children of light in general. Their conduct in such a case would show "in the day of Christ" that his sacrifice of effort had not been in vain. The intensity of this effort can be measured by the figures drawn from a foot race and the toil of a laborer. Paul was happy in his choice of the altar upon which he placed his sacrifices. Even if the price is to be that of life itself, "poured out as a libation," [2] his joy and theirs will continue undiminished.

## III. "THE MASTER'S ERRAND" (vv. 19-30)

The caption for this paragraph is a phrase from the lips of the late Dr. S. D. Gordon. Those who have heard this author of the widely helpful *Quiet Talks* will remember how he spoke frequently of being "on the Master's errand." No one in a place of leadership like that which the apostle Paul occupied can do the work alone. There must be those whom he can send and who find in their mission the satisfaction of being identified, not with the human leader, but with the Sender in supreme command. Timothy and Epaphroditus felt this sense of mission, and are numbered in the delightful fellowship

---

[2] A. T. Robertson, *Word Pictures in the New Testament*, IV, 447.

of those who set forward the gospel by subordinating their convenience to its claims.

### 1. *Timothy* (vv. 19-24)

Timothy had come with Paul on his first visit to Philippi and had been in constant attendance upon the great apostle throughout all his hardships since. Verse 19 explains the purpose of his contemplated mission. Paul hoped to send him in the very near future for a quick trip to Philippi that, as a result of this visit, he himself might be of good comfort by knowing how they fared. Timothy's qualifications for this mission are given in verses 20-22. No one of Paul's associates was more like-minded with him than Timothy, or cared more sincerely for the welfare of the Christians in Philippi. His readiness to go and come as their needs might dictate stands in sharp contrast to the rest in Rome, who were busily concerned about their own affairs rather than the things of Christ (v. 21).

There is a touch of severity in this estimate, which must be understood in the light of the Christian imperative. With Paul the needs of the gospel had priority over all other claims, and he was unable to release others from the exacting discipline which he cheerfully accepted for himself. The Philippians could themselves vouch for Timothy's fitness for the task (v. 22). With that delicate consideration for the feeling of others which endeared him forever to his associates, Paul says, "As a child serveth his father, so *with* me he served in furtherance of the gospel" (v. 22 ASV). Timothy was to start out for Philippi just as soon as Paul could see the outcome of his trial. Verse 24 reflects his confidence in the Lord that his acquittal would make it possible for him also to come to them shortly.

## 2. *Epaphroditus* (vv. 25-30)

The case of Epaphroditus was somewhat different. He had come with a gift from the church at Philippi to minister to Paul's needs in prison. On his return trip Epaphroditus would bear this letter of thanks. He was Paul's "brother, fellow-worker, and comrade-in-arms," and their "apostle and minister" to his need (v. 25). Verses 26-28 describe the peculiar urgency the apostle felt in sending him back to Philippi as soon as possible and the joy that would be gained by his return to them safe and sound. Epaphroditus had fallen sick in Rome with an illness that brought him very near death's door. But God had raised him up, showing mercy on him, and on Paul as well, who was thus spared an added sorrow. In the meantime friends back in Philippi had heard about his illness, and the knowledge of their concern made Epaphroditus all the more desirous of getting back to them. All in all, these verses reveal a familiar picture. The ties of Christian love that bind us one to another and to God are the same now as then.

In verses 29-30 Paul bespeaks for Epaphroditus a cordial reception. It is a case of honor bestowed where honor is deserved by one who "staked his life" in a ministry to others. "Paul uses here a gambler's phrase. Epaphroditus gambled with his life in the risk that he ran in coming to Rome, either from the Roman fever or Nero's wrath or some unknown peril." [3] A distinct element in the joy of a Christian is the romance of the uncertain. Faith, however strong, does not rule out the element of risk. The whole scheme of redemption as a grand adventure still beckons to all who will take their chances with God.

---

[3] Robertson, *Paul's Joy in Christ*, p. 172.

### QUESTIONS FOR REVIEW AND EXAMINATION

1. What does "Christ-mindedness" mean in the light of the actions of Jesus described in verses 5-11?
2. In verses 12-18 what three reasons does Paul give to challenge the Philippians to "work out their own salvation," that is, to do their part toward reaching spiritual maturity?
3. In the first paragraph (vv. 1-11) Paul gives several instructions for overcoming divisions in the church. Underline these in your Bible. How many do you find?

# CHAPTER VII

# NEW VALUES FOR OLD

## PHILIPPIANS 3:1-21

The river of joy that flows through the book of Philippians is fed by many tributaries. There are two main sources, however, which lie high up in the snow-clad heavenlies. One source, as we have seen, is the thrill of continuous triumph, the exultation of being more than conqueror as hardships and sufferings are made to yield unspeakable privilege. The other main source of joy is found in the third chapter of Philippians, into which we are now entering. It is the thrill of possessing life's greatest treasure. Like the pearl of great price, the very excellence of this treasure calls for a complete revaluation of all things once cherished. There is nothing static, however, in the enjoyment of this possession, as the figure of the pearl and as the complacent attitude of some Christians might suggest. The joy of gaining Christ unfolds, rather, as a holy quest.

The joy section of the letter (Phil. 1:12 to 3:21) merges with the peace section described in Philippians 4. However, Philippians 3:1 and Philippians 4:4, by their familiar and joyous refrain, seem in a general way to mark the logical beginning and ending of the passage under discussion and to justify the approach we have taken in this chapter on "New Values for Old."

## I. A CAROL BREAKS INTO CAUTION (vv. 1-4)

Paul appears on the point of closing his letter with a song of joy. "Finally, my brethren, rejoice in the Lord" (Phil. 3:1 ASV). The fact that he continues to write almost as much again beyond the word "finally" as he had written before it indicates the free and informal nature of the note of thanks he had intended to write from the first. "Finally, my brethren" means about what it means when some preachers use it in the middle of their discourse. Its temporal quality is not to be taken too seriously! "To keep on writing the same thing to you," Paul says, "for me is not tedious (in the least), and for you it is safe" (v. 1). Westcott and Hort, in their edition of the Greek text, indicate the break which occurs at this point by closing the brief paragraph with a dash. His song of joy ceases abruptly as the song of a bird that has suddenly seen the shadow of a circling hawk. When Paul thinks of their safety, he thinks of their danger also, and interrupts his song to deal with that danger in caustic words of caution.

Verse 2 warns against the false teachings of the Judaizers, whereas verse 3 points out the true position of the Christian. There is a cumulative effect in this repetition. Paul says, "Beware . . . beware . . . beware," as though he would build a threefold barrier to keep the believer on the highway of truth. The danger against which he gives this sharp caution, however, is the danger of being attacked rather than that of turning from the truth.

The vicious nature of the enemy is revealed in the words "dogs," "evil-workers," and "concision." If these terms seem strong, one must remember how Paul had suffered from his adversaries among the Jews who insisted with such vehemence that it was necessary for believers to assume the burden of Jewish legalism along with their responsibilities as Christians. Paul recognized the malice which prompted these "evil workers."

He called them "dogs" partly because from time immemorial that had been a term of contempt among the

Jews and partly because it was so descriptive of the way they worked, snarling and snapping at his heels or attacking his converts whenever his back was turned. The translators have made a fairly successful effort to bring over Paul's play on words by the use of "concision." So intent were these Judaizers on this knifing business that they mutiliated entirely the meaning which lay in the Jewish rite of circumcision. The church at Philippi apparently had suffered less than others from these enemies of Paul, but the threat was ever present, and they would do well to heed his caution.

In striking contrast to these false teachers, Paul asserts his own position. He includes the Philippians with himself in the use of the pronoun "we," which stands for emphasis at the beginning of the sentence (v. 3). "*We* are the [true] circumcision who serve in God's Spirit and make our boast in Christ Jesus, and have no reliance on flesh—though for my part I could beat them at their own game even there!" All that is fine and true in Judaism— or any other religion for that matter—is found in its noblest form in the gospel of Jesus. The fact is that Paul fulfilled his noblest heritage as a Jew by becoming a Christian, if his adversaries could only have seen it.

But they were blind to spiritual values. They wanted to make a good showing before others so that they could boast in appearance and numbers. Paul's words of caution should put us on guard against those whose glorying in the flesh inflates the ego. We must remember that glorying is directional (Rom. 4:2)—the direction in which it points will reveal whether it stems from the flesh or from the Spirit. Paul's sharp caution is needed today that our boasting may be such as to point men to Jesus and not to ourselves.

## II. REVISED ESTIMATES OF WORTH (vv. 5-16)

The finest protection which life affords is a true sense of values. Realizing that caution against certain dangers amounts to little unless one is equipped to meet them, Paul proceeds in the paragraph before us to present Christ as the criterion by which all values are to be determined. In sacred intimacy he opens up his own heart-life to let us see the delicate processes of discernment whereby supreme worth becomes his motivation in the quest of life.

The key word, occurring three times in verses 7 and 8, is the word "count." The picture in the Greek verb so translated is that of something standing foremost after a considered estimate has been made. Our English word "count," close kin to "compute," serves admirably to bring this idea into the workaday world with which we are familiar. After all, the success of any business is determined by the values which are exchanged across the "counter," and to this principle, Paul says, the business of living is no exception. Jesus gives to life a higher meaning than can be found elsewhere. Every experience yields surpassing value when interpreted by him as the standard. Paul's own life had been immeasurably enriched by this discovery which he longs to share with others.

### 1. *Things That Once Were Gain* (vv. 5-7)

Paul had this advantage over the Judaizers. He could meet them on their own footing and prove from his own experience as a Jew the superiority of a life that recognized Jesus as the Messiah and grace as the fulfilment of the law. He set down in calculated order the values held supreme by their standards: the values which were his by right of birth ("circumcised the eighth day, of the stock of Israel, of the tribe of Benjamin, a Hebrew of the Hebrews"); the values which were his by right of party affiliation (identified in the interpretation of the law with the loyally orthodox Pharisees, who, in contrast to the skeptical Sadducees, preserved the hope of Israel in their belief of the supernatural); the values which were his by right of experience (zeal for the cause prompting him to ask on his own initiative [Acts 9:2] for warrants of arrest in his persecution of the church); and the values which were his by right of moral integrity (since, measured by the law, he was found blameless).

No one can lightly set aside such assets as these. Together they constituted Paul's position in the world of his day. Whatever a man's advantages may be, they avail nothing if he is not in position to use them. The finest equipment means nothing to the hunter who is not in a position to use his gun when the bird is flushed. We must remember this importance of position in order to appreciate presently the advantage which Paul found "in Christ" (v. 9).

### 2. *The Radical Revision* (vv. 7-8)

In verses 7-8 Paul indicates that there has been a complete upsetting of his scale of values. Something has happened to revise all former standards. "The old things are passed away; behold, they are become new" (2 Cor. 5:17 ASV). The force of the atom bomb was not in its physical violence alone, but in the fact that as a new weapon it made previous methods of warfare obsolete.

The new power in Paul's life is utterly devastating to the old way in which he has lived. "Howbeit, what gains I then thought were mine, these have I, after deliberate consideration, set down as loss because of Christ" (Phil. 3:7). The next verse repeats this statement and amplifies it by extending it in several directions. He enlarges "such things as were gains to me" to include "all things"; he expands "for Christ" to mean "for the excellency of the knowledge of Christ Jesus my Lord"; he deepens the contrast by using the word "refuse" (or "offal," such as might be flung to the dogs) for "loss"; and, finally, he underscores it all by reference to his own experience, stating that he has stood the loss and found the gain and is more than delighted with the results. To Paul, Christ makes all the difference in the world.

No one who has laid down all things for Christ ever seems dissatisfied with the exchange. On the contrary, those who have done so seem possessed of a joy unknown to others. A missionary with more than forty years of experience in China was speaking once to a small group gathered in the midweek service of prayer. He had been talking about the incident in Simon's home at Bethany when Mary anointed the Saviour with her costly ointment. The breaking of the alabaster flask symbolized an utterness of devotion which gave wings to the Word. "There are some Christians," he said, "who do not know what it is to give their all for Christ." His eyes grew moist, and he added with becoming modesty, "But I think I do, and I am sorry for those who don't." They were the ones who had missed the greater gain.

### 3. *Gaining Christ* (vv. 9-14)

We have seen that Paul has a good deal to say about profit and loss. In previous verses he has described those things which, according to his new standard of reckoning, he has charged off as loss. He continues now in the next several verses to enlarge upon the measureless gain which is his in Christ. The idea is summed up in the one word "Christ" (v. 7) and again in the phrase, "the excellency of the knowledge of Christ Jesus my Lord" (v. 8 ASV). Dividends from his new treasure accumulate so rapidly that in an effort to describe them he uses words which say, in effect, "One discovery continually surpasses another in the delights of my experience with him."

What he means by "gaining Christ" is expanded to include three ideas developed in the following verses.

(1) *A new position* (v. 9).—When Paul received Christ, he gained the advantage of a new position and felt immediately the security which it afforded. The phrase "in Christ" is a favorite expression with Paul, who uses it or some similar expression such as "in the Lord" or "in him" 164 times. We are told that it is Paul the mystic who speaks thus, but that need not baffle us, for all of us are mystics in the sense that there are some things we know through a process more direct than that of reasoning. It is this immediacy that makes a mystic. Jesus was the greatest mystic of all; yet we understand perfectly what he means when he says, "I am the vine, ye are the branches: He that abideth in me, and I in him, the same beareth much fruit: for apart from me ye can do nothing" (John 15:5 ASV).

Our safety lies in our position "in Christ," but our fruitfulness lies in the extent to which Christ is in us. Paul declared that "Christ in you" is the "hope of glory" (Col. 1:27 ASV). To him, a man was either out of Christ or in Christ. The relationship is a living, fruit-bearing one like that between the vine and the branch. In making Christ's death effective within the believer, the Holy Spirit cuts him away from the old source of life which was his by nature and, through the quickening power of the resurrection, skilfully grafts him into a new Source of life which thenceforth is to find expression in a fruitfulness flavored by the believer's own individuality.

After this process the branch is indeed dead to the old source of life and alive only to the new. Paul teaches all this in the beautiful symbolism of baptism. Our difficulty sometimes is that we look at that ordinance too much from the manward side. We forget that from God's point of view it represents the way we become living members of the body of Christ (1 Cor. 12:13), and that this is the greatest privilege of all.

We have had several occasions to remark previously on the importance of one's position. God's very first question to fallen man, "Where art thou?" was designed to help him discover his position (Gen. 3:9). The scene in the garden of Eden comes to mind in connection with Paul's statement here, "That I may . . . be found in him, not having a righteousness of mine own, even that which is of the law, but that which is through faith in Christ, the righteousness which is from God by faith" (Phil. 3:9 ASV).

The tense and the voice in the verb "found" combine to indicate a sudden disclosure that will reveal in naked truth exactly *where* a man is and *what* he is. Paul confidently hopes that such a revealing will not be embarrassing to him, as it was to our first parents after their sin in the garden of Eden. He has cast aside the fig leaves of a righteousness wrought through his own efforts to keep the law and stands clothed in the seamless robe of that righteousness which is from God by faith in Christ.

> When he shall come with trumpet sound,
> Oh, may I then in Him be found;
> Dressed in His righteousness alone,
> Faultless to stand before the throne.
>
> EDWARD MOTE

(2) *A new fellowship* (vv. 10-11).—A part of Paul's gain in Christ was to know him in terms of his resurrection power: "To know him and the power of his resurrection and the fellowship of his sufferings, becoming

[day by day] conformed to his death; if somehow [in the process] I might attain unto [the maximum experience of] his resurrection from the dead" (v. 10). Each part of this statement challenges prayerful study. One cannot speak dogmatically about the application of certain ideas advanced here. Paul wanted to know a living Lord whose mastery of death in all of its forms is complete. In Ephesians 1:19 he refers to "the exceeding greatness of his power to us-ward who believe" (ASV). He was fully aware that resurrection power is available only to those who approach it by way of death. He recognized that there must be in him a continual conformity to the pattern laid down in Christ's death. Only thus could life come. There is nothing morbid in this approach, for the cross was for him the gateway to privilege and power.

There is no fellowship as sweet as that which one has with friends in their suffering. We share our joys with many, our sorrows with only a privileged few of our friends; and it is that way with God. It was the favored three whom Jesus took with him into the deeper shades of Gethsemane. Paul had come to know Christ in the sacred intimacy of his sufferings as he could have known him in no other way, and he counted the experience a privilege.

We are puzzled by Paul's statement, "If by any means I may attain unto the resurrection from the dead" (v. 11 ASV). The context of all his teaching brooks no uncertainty concerning the resurrection. Grammatically, the construction permits the idea of a difference in rank or order to which he aspires in the day of resurrection. The phrase "each in his own order" (1 Cor. 15:23 ASV) is one of a few passages which seem to fall in with this conception.

It is not illogical that in a day of giving rewards some

should take precedence over others, like honor students in commencement exercises. But in following this interpretation one may become liable to the mistake which Martha made in her interview with Jesus after the death of her brother Lazarus. She believed that her brother would rise again in the resurrection at the last day, but found scant comfort in it (John 11:24).

Matters were quite different, however, when Jesus showed her that the resurrection was not a day but a Person. "*I* am the resurrection, and the life," he said (John 11:25 ASV). In taking hold upon this fresh revelation of Jesus, her faith brought that resurrection power into glorious manifestation. We may be sure that Paul was more concerned with a continuing demonstration of such a power than he was with a day marked on the calendar of God.

(3) *A new purpose* (vv. 12-14).—Christ brought to Paul the tremendous gain of something worth living for, a goal worthy of all the marvelous capacities of his being. This is of priceless value. Without a worthy goal life becomes listless, and one falls a prey to Satan's most devastating question, "What's the use?" Any obstacle can be surmounted by one who has glimpsed the prize and knows it to be worth all the struggle it costs, and more.

Paul's procedure in stating this new purpose which Christ has brought to him reminds us of that which we have already noted in verses 7 and 8. The two sentences in verses 12 and 13-14 state almost exactly the same thing, but verses 13-14 enlarge greatly upon the statement made in verse 12: "Not that I have already obtained, or am already made perfect: but I press on, if so be that I may lay hold on that for which also I was laid hold on by Christ Jesus" (ASV).

He has felt the grip of the Master's hand upon his shoulder and has devoted the whole of his being to realizing the purpose Christ had in mind when he laid such firm hold upon him. The intensity of Paul's spirit is revealed by the restatement of these very same truths in the next two verses. He reaches further into the resources of his own being and into the grace of God to pour every ounce of energy into the process of achievement. That which Christ had in mind in laying hold upon him becomes more definitely a goal, continually challenging as it beckons upward, "the prize of the high calling of God in Christ Jesus." The recognition of his own shortcoming has become a fixed attitude of humility.

God has blessed him richly since he turned on the Damascus road to take orders from his new Lord, but he has not yet "arrived." His maturity is marked by a realization of his immaturity, as we shall see in verse 15. Thus, inspired by the margin between himself and such a goal, he concentrates his energies and throws himself into the race before him.

There is wholesome psychology in this passage for those of us who must live under tension. Paul's enjoyment of life and his effectiveness lay in no small part in his ability to concentrate upon the one thing in hand. Many a Christian has allowed a sense of thronging duties to distract his attention from the one task in hand and thus to subtract from the joy the task should yield to him and also from the results it should yield to those whom he is trying to serve. Jesus said there were twelve hours in every man's day (John 11:9), indicating that there was time enough for every man to do the task God has assigned. The Christian has no business with anything else, and will find himself out from under a great strain when he realizes it.

Paul's words about "forgetting the things which are behind" are good psychology, too. In Philippians 1:3 he said, "I thank my God upon all my remembrance of you"

(ASV). It takes a healthy mind to remember that which helps and to forget that which hinders, but such a mind is our privilege in Christ. In this connection one thinks of Sir William Osler's very sound advice. "The load of to-morrow added to that of yesterday, carried today, makes the strongest falter." Long before Osler's day, Paul found the joy of this secret.

### 4. *The Norm of Maturity* (vv. 15-16)

He who has just denied perfection (v. 12) now numbers himself among the perfect (v. 15). The apparent contradiction is removed by an understanding of the word translated "perfect." The idea involved is one of maturity. Paul regards himself as spiritually adult (1 Cor. 13:11) and associates others with himself in that category. But it is the mark of the mature mind to recognize that there is yet much to learn. Only the fool knows it all, and he quickly reveals his folly by being so cocksure.

Another token of Paul's maturity is in the generous allowance he makes for the brother who might be otherwise-minded, for the adverb he uses means "differently." Even in such a case, if his attitude is humble, God will show him better in due time. The point is to keep on stepping (a different word from that usually translated "walk") where the light falls brightest. "Only, where-unto we have attained, by that same rule let us walk" (v. 16 ASV). There must be no slipping back.

### III. THE HEAVENLY CITIZENSHIP (vv. 17-21)

Verse 17 marks a gradual transition into the final para-graph of Philippians 3. In this section we see Paul and others as examples of those who have, so to speak, "come of age" in the heavenly citizenship (v. 17); we contrast the tragic lot of those who, through their enmity to the cross, refuse to take out citizenship in the heavenly kingdom (vv. 18-19); and we are gladdened by the prospects of a returning Saviour, the Lord Jesus Christ, whose rule is supreme and whose presence among his subjects will mean indescribable joy.

## 1. *Paul, the Example* (v. 17)

"Become imitators of me, brethren, and pay close attention to those who so walk, even as ye have us for an example." Those who know Paul's spirit will take no offense at that which might at first seem to others almost an immodest statement. Paul invites the Philippians to imitate (our "mimic" is derived from the word he uses) him and holds himself up as a type or example for them to follow. Like the teacher who writes the copy upon the blackboard, Paul points to the pattern of his own life.

It is not Paul's sense of modesty at fault, however, but our own if we take exception to what he said. He faces up to the fact that he is an example and shoulders the responsibility of such a position, while we, behind a false modesty, often try to evade the fact that whether we like it or not, someone is imitating us. Actually we have no choice between being an example and not being one; we can only choose between being a good example and being a bad one. More than we are aware we set the pattern for others to follow. True humility quietly accepts this responsibility and looks to God for grace to be the kind of example that others may well follow.

## 2. *Enemies of the Cross* (vv. 18-19)

In contrast to these whom Paul has held up along with himself as examples are many whom he describes as enemies of the cross. That phrase, of course, could include all who were opposed to the way of Christ, but it seems to apply more directly to some who, posing as Christians, have made license of their professed liberty and have fallen victims to materialism, the rankest idolatry of all. The apostle is about to expose them with the severest words at his command. His right to make such a scathing denunciation lies in the tears which spring to his eyes as he thinks upon the tragedy of their way. It is heartbreaking to think how many materialists there are whose names are on our church rolls.

In verse 19 Paul gives four characteristics of these enemies of the cross, whatever their professions otherwise might be.

"Their end is perdition." Let there be no doubt in anyone's mind about that. Paul uses a word that describes the direct antithesis of salvation. It is a hard thing to get some church members to see that they are on the road to hell, but the faithful minister of the gospel will try.

"Their god is their belly." What they can eat, what they can put on, what contributes to their comfort and their convenience, means more to them than anything else. These considerations determine their habits and their outlook on life. The golden calf has been cast into a different form today. Pointing to the gadgets and conveniences which pour from our assembly lines and all the luxuries which make for an easy life, a voice says to America, "These be thy gods, O Israel" (Ex. 32:4).

Such an outlook can but supply the next characteristic: "Their glory is in their shame." Man must boast in something; and if he does not know the Lord, all that in which he prides himself will one day prove his embarrassment.

To the casual reader, the fourth mark of these enemies of the cross may come somewhat as an anticlimax. "Who mind earthly things" seems mild by comparison with "whose end is perdition." But the sentence builds up to stress the greatest danger of all. Like carbon monoxide gas, this frame of mind is all the more lethal because it is so often undetected. It settles upon a man before he is aware that his drowsiness to things spiritual presages the sleep of death. Paul's expression reminds us of what our Lord said to Peter, who also protested against the cross: "Get thee behind me, Satan . . . thou mindest not the things of God, but the things of men" (Matt. 16:23 ASV). Enemies of the cross can never become citizens of the heavenly kingdom.

## 3. *The Coming of the King* (vv. 20-21)

Somewhat by way of anticipation we have applied Paul's mention of the heavenly citizenship in verse 20 to the preceding verses of this paragraph. This procedure seems justified by the marked emphasis which rests on "our citizenship," in contrast to the "many" whose walk in life Paul has deplored in verses 18-19.

The Philippians would have been quick to appreciate the force of Paul's figure of speech when he said, "Our citizenship belongs all the while in heaven." Roman citizenship meant a great deal both to Paul and to them. It had served Paul in good stead when the praetors were on the point of shrugging off their mistreatment of him and Silas (Acts 16:37). It also afforded the Philippians the advantages which their city enjoyed as a colony of Rome (Acts 16:12). The analogy was most appropriate and affords a lesson for all believers. The local church should be like a colony of heaven—heavenly laws and heavenly manners should mark its members as different from others about them.

The greatest event in any colony of Rome was a visit from the emperor. History records the most elaborate honors for such an occasion. Coins were struck, new highways were built, magnificent public buildings were erected, and imperial favors were bestowed by way of celebration. Looking forward to such an event, the Christian colony has something infinitely glorious in prospect in the coming of the Lord Jesus Christ. Our humble dwellings—these frail bodies—will be fashioned anew to match the splendor of his own resurrection body according to the working of the imperial might which marks him as sovereign of the universe (v. 21).

Down through the centuries these words have poured their consolation into countless weary hearts by the open grave. Many a saint has watched the valiant fight of a loved one struggling against the ravages of disease—struggling well but in vain. In a way every death is a defeat. That is why Paul calls the mortal body "the body of our humiliation." It is not "vile," as the King James Version puts it—certainly not in the sense in which we use that word today. It is "the body of our low estate," subject to disease, death, and decay.

But it has a glorious destiny in the eyes of our Redeemer. At his coming it will be fashioned anew and brought into complete conformity to the body of his glory. Death will be swallowed up in victory (1 Cor. 15:54). Paul wisely does not say how this is to be. By faith he has experienced the working of a power which is to him the guarantee of Christ's ability to bring this last enemy and all things else in subjection to himself, and he rests in the radiant joy of such assurance.

### QUESTIONS FOR REVIEW AND EXAMINATION

1. Make a list of the advantages, mentioned in verses 4-7, which Paul counted as important before he knew Christ. Next to it list all the things which he mentions in verses 8-11 as the things he now considers of greatest value in life.

2. What is meant by the expression "spiritually adult"? What word in verse 15 has this meaning? From verses 12-16 list some characteristics of a mature Christian.

3. Paul called some professing Christians "enemies of the cross." In verses 18-19 find four characteristics of such people. State these characteristics in present-day terms.

4. What encouraging message has Paul in verses 20-21 for the citizens of heaven as they live on earth?

# CHAPTER VIII

# PEACE, PERFECT PEACE

### PHILIPPIANS 4:1-23

It frequently happens when a symphony nears its end that the listener will be reminded of themes already developed in preceding movements, phrases of which are woven into the finale, which in the case of Philippians, instead of building up to a mighty crescendo, flows into the calm of heavenly harmony. Many truths which have already been expressed in this letter will come up again, and we shall find that some of them can be developed more fittingly here than in earlier passages.

We have seen that this epistle can be considered in three sections: the *love passage* (1:1-11), the *joy passage* (1:12 to 3:21), and the *peace passage* (4:1-23). From the very nature of these emotions—love, joy, and peace—we shall not be surprised to find love and joy overflowing in the peace section of the epistle. The charm of the letter to the Philippians is due to the perfect blend of these virtues rather than to a separate analysis of each. However, the peace of God which this epistle brings to our troubled hearts is the crown jewel of all the treasures of grace.

According to the editors of the American Standard Version there are seven paragraphs in the fourth chapter of Philippians. The rather decided break between verses 7 and 8 is wholly a matter of their own opinion. Westcott and Hort do not even make a new paragraph in the Greek text at that point. The unity of the chapter will be better preserved if we keep in mind the underlying thought of peace. In the over-all message Paul seems to be saying, "Be at peace one with another; be at peace within your own hearts; be at peace with the surroundings in which your lot is cast." However lest we superimpose any artificial pattern of our own, we shall do well to gather our impressions around headings suggested by the major paragraphs themselves.

## I. EUODIA AND SYNTYCHE (vv. 1-3)

The apostle pauses in verse 1 both to repeat the old refrain of love and joy and to link the bright hope of the Christian, which he has just described, with the responsibilities of the present in a most practical sort of way. The "wherefore" is characteristic of Paul's practice of relating the thought of Christ's return to the task immediately at hand. If in that day they are to be his "crown" as they are now his "joy," they must keep the resolute stand in the Lord which they have taken. Love and longing, pride and joy, add their warmth to the logic of this appeal (v. 1).

### 1. *Careful Impartiality* (v. 2)

The next two verses fairly throb with human interest. We know nothing about Euodia and Syntyche except what is told us here. They were two good women who had shown splendid teamwork [1] in the gospel with Paul and others whom he classed as his "fellow-workers." The meaning of their names is interesting, though wholly incidental. "Euodia" means "fragrant." The same word is translated in verse 18 as "sweet smell": "an odor of a sweet smell, a sacrifice acceptable, well-pleasing to

---

[1] The word translated "labored" is the same as that translated "strive" in Philippians 1:27. The picture is that of an athlete playing his part on a team.

God" (ASV). "Syntyche" has the idea of our "good luck," "fortunate."

We can but wonder about the disagreement between these two women. Whatever its nature, it was well-known in the church at Philippi, for Paul felt no hesitancy in dealing with it publicly. Perhaps a certain amount of jealousy was involved, as is frequently the case in feuds which mar the fellowship of a church. At any rate Paul proceeds with careful impartiality: "Euodia I exhort, and Syntyche I exhort, be thinking the same thing in the Lord" (v. 2). He goes back again to Christ-mindedness, which is the answer to every rift that may occur among Christians. In a church it is as with an orchestra where the instruments are in tune one with another only because each has been first tuned to standard pitch. Reconciliation among church members takes place quickly enough when each becomes attuned to Christ. Getting right and keeping right with him is the Christian's first business always.

## 2. *An Interesting Aside* (v. 3)

In a lecture to a class on Philippians, the late Dr. W. Hersey Davis made the suggestion that Paul turned aside as he dictated this letter to address either Timothy or Epaphroditus as "true yokefellow," and to charge him to "help these women." Then the amanuensis, or secretary, incorporated this side remark with the letter itself. Westcott and Hort indicate by a marginal reading that the word translated "yokefellow" is itself a proper name. "He requests Syzygus (lit. = joiner · together) to help Euodia and Syntyche to make up their differences." [2] At least it was a term of address sufficiently understood by the church at Philippi to assign the responsibility to some particular individual. The women who publish

[2] *The Expositor's Greek Testament*, III, 466.

the tidings are a great host in our churches and need
more help from the men than they are getting. Paul
encourages the whole church to work together as a unit.
"Clement must have been some disciple at Philippi, unknown to Church history like the others mentioned
here." [3]  But it is an honor to be enrolled with him and
with all like him who have striven in the furtherance of
the gospel. Their names are in God's book of life.

## II. THE PEACE OF GOD AND THE GOD OF PEACE (vv. 4-9)

It is difficult to find one caption elastic enough to slip
around these next verses and strong enough to hold them
together without doing violence to the natural independence of some of them. The underlying flow of thought
almost defies analysis. This difficulty is noticeable in
verse 4 and again between verses 7 and 8. Paul has
touched upon the joy of those whose names are written
in the book of heaven (Luke 10:20), and the occasion
is sufficient to introduce again the familiar theme. "Rejoice in the Lord always: again I will say, Keep on rejoicing" (v. 4). After this introduction the underlying
movement of his thought becomes a little easier to trace.
It is the flow of God's own kind of peace.

### 1. *The Peace of God* (vv. 5-7)

The peace which Paul describes in the following verses
surges through the human heart outward toward our
fellow men. It springs from a sense of God's nearness
and the practice of a face-to-face praying in which
everything is laid out in the open before him. Its quality
surpasses all human understanding, and there is about
it the strength of an armed guard which is its own guarantee of preservation. In this day of tension and trouble,

[3] *Ibid.*, III, 466.

of frustration and failure, when pressure increases to the breaking point, we shall do well to linger with these verses long enough to learn their secret.

(1) *Its outflow to others* (v. 5).—"Let your forbearance be known to all men" (ASV), says the apostle. Matthew Arnold finds in the word translated "forbearance" "a pre-eminent feature in the character of Jesus and designates it 'sweet reasonableness.'" [4] When once the peace of God acts as umpire in the Christian's heart (Col. 3:15), others will find him of all men most fairminded and sweetly reasonable. It is a shame when a person charged with the ministry of reconciliation allows an overbearing and unreasonable spirit to cripple his efforts. Before a man can bring peace to others, he must be at peace with himself and within himself.

(2) *Its wellsprings* (vv. 5-6).—There are two wellsprings to God's kind of peace: the sense of his nearness and the practice of prayer. Fear and anxiety are dissipated in the realization of Christ's presence. The disciples were frightened in the storm on Galilee because they had not yet realized who was present with them in the boat. They knew him, but not as he was to be known. Fear, worry, and nervousness are all lost in the awareness that one is present who loves us and whose resources are those of infinite wisdom and power.

But this awareness cannot be ours without cultivation on our part. The windows of the soul must be kept open toward God by prayer. "In nothing be anxious; but in everything by means of prayer and supplication, in an atmosphere of thanksgiving let your requests become known face-to-face with God" (v. 6). Every word in this classic sentence will repay careful study. As is so often the case, the prepositions reveal a wealth of meaning. "In everything"—nothing is too small, nothing

---

[4] *Ibid.*, III, 466.

too great, to lay before him. The general word for "prayer" is particularized by the use of "requests," which has about it the "cry of personal need."

The use of the preposition "with" (from which our "mid" is derived) conveys the idea of an atmosphere of praise and thanksgiving in the midst of which we present our supplication. The picture in the preposition "before" ("unto" in the King James Version) is that of being face-to-face with God. In the constant exercise of such a privilege there is small wonder that fears will flee and peace pervade the sanctuary of the human heart.

(3) *Its might and mystery* (v. 7).—The figure Paul uses in verse 7 reminds us of the words of Jesus: "When the strong man fully armed guardeth his own court, his goods are in peace" (Luke 11:21 ASV). The peace of God is not of a negative quality. It is not soft with compromise and appeasement. Toward the threat of Satan and all the minions of hell it is hard as nails; it is made up of the spikes of the cross and blood, and empty cerements of death, and a seal broken in defiance of Imperial Rome. It is the peace of superior might, the calm of absolute adequacy.

During the revolution of China in 1911, a small boy was fleeing with his missionary parents from the interior to safety in Shanghai. For months the troops of the north had passed through the city where he had lived on their way to the front. Alarming rumors of bloodshed and disorder had filled his heart with anxiety. The train on which his parents and a few other missionaries were riding was by special permission to pass through the lines en route to Hankow. He saw the opposing armies drawn up in battle array, and the bullet scars on the buildings when he arrived in Hankow. That night the city was quiet. The fighting had passed farther north, and a contingent of British soldiers, supported by a warship standing by on the Yangtse River, had things in hand. Outside his window the measured tread of a British guard assured him that he and his loved ones could rest in perfect safety, and all fear was gone as he lay down to sleep.

God is like that. He sets a garrison of peace to stand guard over our hearts and our thoughts in Christ Jesus.

This further word, however, should be said about the mystery of a peace that "passeth all understanding." Such a peace is really quite different from that which many people carelessly think it is. They think they want the peace that passeth all understanding, but actually what they want is a peace that is very easily understood. They want the peace that grows out of the tranquility of their surroundings, the pastoral scene where all goes well, the peace of being made to lie down in green pastures and being led beside the still waters. The peace Paul had in mind was past all understanding because it was his amid tempestuous surroundings, amid riot and storm, and under the threat of the headsman's ax.

In a little pamphlet Miss Marie Monsen, a Norwegian missionary to China, has related her experience as a captive for twenty-three days on a ship commandeered by pirates in April, 1929. She unfolds an amazing testimony of God's faithfulness during all those days when her life was in constant danger from the robbers who looted and plundered the junks and fishing craft that plied the waters near Tientsin.

One would expect that such a harrowing experience would seem like a hideous nightmare to the lone foreign woman among the passengers held prisoners by more than fifty pirates. The title she gave to her message, however, was *Resting in God's Faithfulness.* She found the peace that passeth all understanding. Yet one wonders how many of those in search for peace of mind today would care to find it through adversity as she did.

### 2. And the God of Peace (vv. 8-9)

Paul closed this paragraph with the promise that God would be with them. God's presence would guarantee the perpetuation of his peace, but the promise of that presence is conditioned on two things: their own thought-life (v. 8) and the continued practice of the lessons Paul had given them through his own example (v. 9). The two go hand in hand: "Keep thinking upon these things . . . keep practicing these things." A peaceful heart, therefore, does not come by magic. How it can exist in such circumstances as those which surrounded Paul may be a mystery to some, but when once the secret is learned, it will be found that God fulfils the laws of sound psychology and good religion in bringing it about.

In verse 8 God's garrison of peace is to stand guard over our *thoughts* as well as our hearts. We are to receive only those thoughts that he permits. But such is God's respect for our own integrity as individuals that his guard cannot turn away the guests we welcome. Each of us determines what he will think about, and God challenges us in this text to face up to that responsibility. "For as he thinketh within himself, so is he" (Prov. 23:7 ASV).

The lovely virtues named in verse 8 gleam like pearls threaded on a golden chain. These are the things to reflect upon: "Whatsoever things are true, whatsoever things are honorable [of a nature to awaken reverence], whatsoever things are just [right], whatsoever things are pure, [holy, unsullied], whatsoever things are lovely, whatsoever things are of good report, if there be any virtue [moral excellence], and if there be any praise, think on these things" (v. 8 ASV). But it takes practice—

not so much in long hours of contemplation as in down-to-earth living after the example so clearly set by Paul. "The things which ye both learned and received and heard and saw in me, these things do [practice]: and the God of peace shall be with you" (v. 9 ASV).

## III. THE LOVE OFFERING (vv. 10-20)

In the closing paragraph of his letter Paul finally gets around to acknowledging the gift from the Philippian church and the ministry which Epaphroditus has rendered in their behalf. "But I rejoice in the Lord greatly, that now at length ye have revived your thought for me," he says, and then hastens to soften the effect of "now at length" by adding, "wherein ye did indeed take thought, but ye lacked opportunity" (v. 10 ASV). This was, of course, the immediate occasion of his writing. There is a priestly flavor to the paragraph, especially pronounced toward the end. Paul receives their gift, but he treats it, not as a thing in itself, but as a symbol of the manner in which God's grace enables his children to triumph over circumstances.

The maturity of a Christian can be measured by his interpretation of circumstances. The light in which he sees them and the construction he places upon them will largely determine whether he is to be their victor or their victim. His interpretation must be communicated to others as their mutual contacts afford him the opportunity. The Philippian love offering afforded Paul such an opportunity, for there is a mutuality in giving and receiving. In his acceptance of a gift the recipient becomes one with the giver. Paul exemplifies the priesthood of the believer in the way he receives their gift and places it upon the altar of their mutual devotion to Christ. He could have received it with thanks as an expression of their love and an answer to his own physical need. Many people thus accept kindnesses from their friends and keep the transaction entirely on the human level. There is a priestly aspect, however, to the ministry of every Christian, and in the exercise of this privilege every circumstance yields its gifts Godward.

### 1. *Its Significance* (vv. 11-17)

Verses 11-17 reveal the sacramental significance of their gift both for Paul and for them. The values involved are so important that we shall do well to consider them carefully from each point of view.

(1) *For Paul* (vv. 11-14).—"Not that I speak in respect of want," he says. He does not hint for more. The negative stands at the first of the sentence for emphasis, to prepare the way for his positive affirmation: "For I have learned in whatsoever state I am, therein to be content" (v. 11 ASV). Paul was probably influenced to a certain degree by the Stoic philosophers in his use of the word translated "content," which according to its derivation actually means "self-sufficient."

The Stoics made a good deal out of the virtue of self-sufficiency or independence of external circumstances. They held that a man should be sufficient in and unto himself in all things. When asked who was the wealthiest, Socrates said, "He who is content with least, for self-sufficiency is nature's wealth." . . . But, though Paul uses the Stoic word, he has more than the Stoic idea. He expressly disclaims this mere self-sufficiency: "Not that we are sufficient of ourselves, to account anything as from ourselves; but our sufficiency is from God" (2 Cor. 3:5).[5]

In verse 12 Paul elaborates this "manly independence" and explains that he came upon its secret as one initiated into a secret order. The verb translated "I learned the secret" is quite different from the one translated "learn"

---

[5] Robertson, *Paul's Joy in Christ,* p. 251.

in the preceding verse. The stem from which it is derived originally meant to "shut" or "close," as when one is blindfolded. The picture is that of a candidate being initiated into one of the mystery cults of which there were many in Paul's day. The truths learned in the process of initiation may be quite simple, but they are revealed only in the experience itself and thus can never become known to outsiders.

Having been duly initiated, Paul is in possession of the happy secret of independence, but it is a secret which he longs to share with others, for he says forthwith, "I am a match for all circumstances through the One whose inflow of power keeps enabling me" (v. 13). This statement crowns them all. We can be sure that anyone who can sincerely make it has come to happy terms with his surroundings and will go on life's way in peace.

(2) *For them* (vv. 15-17).—Having established his own independence as a servant of Christ, and thus his position to accept their gift, not as an object of charity, but as a priest in the house of God, Paul turns to the Philippians and says, "Howbeit ye did well, having fellowship with me in my affliction" (v. 14). He cites their past record to establish the fellowship which they enjoyed from the beginning in this matter of giving and receiving (vv. 15-16).

Paul encourages such practical fellowship in the gospel, not on the basis of their own charitable impulses nor yet on the basis of need—his own or that of those to whom he ministers—but on the basis of a sound business investment in eternal values, where dividends will accrue to them at compound interest through all time to come. This is the scriptural appeal for giving, and businessmen in particular will respond eagerly when once they see that, like Paul, we seek not the gift, but the fruit that increases to their account (v. 17).

## 2. *Its Acceptance* (vv. 18-20)

Paul now acknowledges "receipt in full," which is the meaning of the verb translated "I have all things." [6] With profound satisfaction in what they have done, he places their gift on the altar of Christ and, along with the incense of his own prayers of gratitude, offers it up, "an odor of a sweet smell, a sacrifice acceptable, well-pleasing to God" (v. 18 ASV). If we were better acquainted with the ritual of Old Testament worship, we could appreciate more fully the figure which Paul uses. After the offering had been presented to God, the priest turned to the waiting worshipers to bestow God's blessings of acceptance. This is what Paul does in that verse which so many have committed to memory: "And my God shall supply every need of yours according to his riches in glory in Christ Jesus" (v. 19 ASV). The inner contentment he has found even in the midst of his adverse circumstances will be theirs also, and ours if we avail ourselves of the riches of God's glory in Christ. In the realization of this truth we turn with gratitude overflowing to "God our Father [to whom be] the glory forever and ever. Amen" (v. 20).

## IV. FAREWELLS AND BENEDICTION (vv. 21-23)

In the salutation at the beginning of his letter, Paul included only Timothy with himself, but now his word of farewell is enlarged to take in all the brethren that are with him (in the immediate circle of friends who attended him) and all the saints (in the city of Rome), with

---

[6] Gustav Adolf Deissmann, *Light from the Ancient East*, p. 110.

special mention of those who were of Caesar's household (vv. 21-22).

Those of us who have shared in the study of this lovely letter will want to bow together now for Paul's final benediction. It may help us to remember, before doing so, that the Greek word for grace which he is about to use has survived to this day in our word "charm." There is a charm about this epistle that we would reflect in our attitude to others. By the quality of our own living we would pass on its love and joy and peace to those around us and on out to others in the ever-widening circle of our influence. Our resources for doing so are found in the measureless grace of God. And now: "The grace of the Lord Jesus Christ be with your spirit" (v. 23 ASV).

## QUESTIONS FOR REVIEW AND EXAMINATION

1. Name the three divisions of the book of Philippians. What is the central thought in the third division (Phil. 4:1-23)?

2. What human interest is there in the mention of Euodia and Syntyche? On what basis would harmony be restored between these two good women?

3. What recipe do you find in verses 5-7 for meeting days of tension, trouble, frustration, failure, and increased pressure? Try to state it in your own words. What two rules are given in verses 8-9 for making this recipe effective?

4. For what was Paul expressing thanks in this letter? Explain how Paul "exemplifies the priesthood of the believer" in the way he received the gift of the Philippians.

# BIBLIOGRAPHY

CARVER, W. O. *The Glory of God in the Christian Calling.* Nashville: Broadman Press, 1949.

CHAMBERS, OSWALD. *If Ye Shall Ask.* New York: Grosset and Dunlap, Inc., 1942.

DEISSMANN, GUSTAV ADOLF. *Light from the Ancient East.* London: Hodder and Stoughton, 1910.

KENNEDY, H. A. A. "The Epistle to the Philippians," *The Expositor's Greek Testament,* W. Robertson Nicoll, editor, Vol. III. New York: Dodd, Mead and Company, 1903.

PHILLIPS, J. B. *Letters to Young Churches.* New York: The Macmillan Company, 1947.

RAMSEY, Arthur Michael. *The Glory of God and the Transfiguration of Christ.* New York: Longmans, Green and Company, 1949.

ROBERTSON, A. T. *Epochs in the Life of Paul.* New York: Charles Scribner's Sons, 1909.

————. *Paul's Joy in Christ.* New York: Fleming H. Revell Company, 1917.

————. *Word Pictures in the New Testament.* Nashville: Sunday School Board of the Southern Baptist Convention, 1931.

STEWART, JAMES S. *A Man in Christ.* New York: Harper and Brothers.